TALL TALES
TEST
MATCH
SPECIAL

TALL TALES
TEST MATCH SPECIAL

THE GOOD, THE BAD, AND THE HILARIOUS FROM THE COMMENTARY BOX

JONATHAN AGNEW & PHIL TUFNELL

BOOKS

BBC Books, an imprint of Ebury Publishing,
20 Vauxhall Bridge Road,
London SW1V 2SA

BBC Books is part of the Penguin Random House group of companies
whose addresses can be found at global.penguinrandomhouse.com

This book is published to accompany the radio series entitled
Test Match Special broadcast on BBC Radio 4 and 5 Live Sports Extra.

Head of BBC Radio Sport: Richard Burgess
Commissioning Editor: Richard Maddock
BBC Cricket Producer: Adam Mountford
Executive Producer: Gary Broadhurst

Text by Nick Constable
Text copyright © Jonathan Agnew and Phil Tuffnell 2022
Text Design © Seagulls Design

First published by BBC Books in 2022
Paperback edition published in 2023

www.penguin.co.uk

A CIP catalogue record for this book is available from the British Library

ISBN 9781785947780

Typeset in 10.32/16.08pt Garamond MT Std by Jouve (UK), Milton Keynes
Printed and bound in Great Britain by Clays Ltd, Elcograf S.p.A

The authorised representative in the EEA is Penguin Random House Ireland,
Morrison Chambers, 32 Nassau Street, Dublin D02 YH68

CONTENTS

Dramatis Personae   vii

EARLY STARTS   1

OFF TO A CLUB   27

COUNTY SET – SEVENTIES AND EIGHTIES   53

COUNTY SET – NINETIES AND NOUGHTIES   87

FANTASY *TMS* – ON DEBUT   107

TMS DOWN UNDER   123

TUFFERS ON TOUR   157

SPECIAL SUMMERS – THE AUSSIES IN
    ENGLAND   183

COMMENTARY BOX LEGENDS   217

BOX SEATS   239

BREAKING NEWS ON *TMS*   269

SPOOFS, BLUNDERS AND WIND-UPS   293

Index   318

Dramatis Personae

From the *TMS* Team

Jonathan Agnew – aka Aggers – Leicestershire and England fast bowler with over 650 first-class wickets. Now BBC cricket correspondent, *TMS* elder statesman and commentator.

Phil Tufnell – aka Tuffers – Middlesex and England spin bowler with 121 Test and over 1000 first-class wickets. Now broadcaster and *TMS* summariser.

Isa Guha – Member of England's 2009 World Cup winning squad. Now TV presenter and *TMS* commentator.

Ebony Rainford-Brent – Member of England's 2009 World Cup winning team and the first black woman to play for England. Now Director of Women's Cricket at Surrey and *TMS* summariser.

Carlos Brathwaite – West Indies T20 captain and all-rounder with 88 T20, ODI and Test caps. Now *TMS* summariser.

Alison Mitchell – *TMS's* first career female commentator and leading BBC Sport reporter.

Aatif Nawaz – *TMS* commentator, cricket lover and award-winning British-Pakistani actor, writer, TV presenter and comedian.

Key characters from *TMS's Tall Tales*

John Arlott – broadcasting great whose poetic ball-by-ball commentary featured on *TMS* between 1957 and 1980.

Mike Atherton – England captain, technically outstanding opening bat who amassed more than 7700 Test runs.

Baggy Bagshaw – opened the bowling with Aggers at his first village club – Ufford Park CC, Stamford. Despite having only one eye, Baggy was unerringly accurate.

Trevor Bailey – England all-rounder and determinedly concise *TMS* summariser.

Jack Bannister – Warwickshire bowler turned cricket commentator who achieved the rare feat of spoofing Aggers in a TV 'interview'.

Peter Baxter – *TMS* producer who somehow managed to keep the show on the road for 34 years.

Don Bennett – Middlesex head coach who first signed Tuffers as a full-time pro cricketer.

Henry Blofield – aka Blowers – a *TMS* commentary great and favourite spoofing target for Aggers.

Geoffrey Boycott – Outstanding England opening bat with over 8000 Test runs. A *TMS* summariser whose well-worn phrases were eagerly anticipated by listeners playing so-called Boycott Bingo.

Richie Benaud – Australia captain, all-rounder and later masterly, if oft-mimicked, TV cricket commentator.

David Constant – Leading English umpire who no-balled Aggers' first delivery in county cricket.

Jeremy Coney – New Zealand medium pace bowler and guest *TMS* summariser.

Hansie Cronje – disgraced South Africa captain at the centre of match-fixing scandals.

Phil DeFreitas – Leicestershire and England all-rounder who played with both Aggers and Tuffers.

Nancy Doyle – much-loved Lord's head cook known for her feisty approach to interference by players and officials.

Roddy Estwick – Carlos's PE teacher and 'father figure' at Combermere Secondary School, Barbados. He later became a West Indies assistant coach.

John Emburey – England and Middlesex spinner who together with Tuffers was one of the Middlesex 'spin twins' of the seventies and eighties.

Duncan Fletcher – England coach who formed a successful Test partnership with England skipper Michael Vaughan. Became something of a *bete noire* for Tuffers however.

Gus Fraser – Reliable, accurate England and Middlesex fast-medium bowler who became one of Tuffers' closest friends in the Middlesex dressing room.

Bill Frindall – long-serving *TMS* scorer credited with inventing the modern system of scoring.

Mike Gatting – England and Middlesex captain, who scored over 4400 Test runs. The man who persuaded a rebellious Tuffers to adopt a more professional approach to cricket.

Graham Gooch – Outstanding England and Essex opener who captained both club and country and scored 8900 Test runs.

Alf Gover – Surrey and England fast bowler who ran an acclaimed coaching school in Wandsworth, London, attended by Aggers.

David Gower – One of the English game's classiest stroke-makers with over 8000 Test runs. Aggers' England and Leicestershire captain and occasional England team-mate of Tuffers.

Kaush Guha – Isa's big brother. She attributes much of her bowling success to being cajoled into bowling at him for hours in their garden.

Ken Higgs – Leicestershire fast bowler, captain and a mentor of Aggers during his early years of county cricket.

Gordon Jenkins – One of Tuffers' long-suffering coaches in the Middlesex youth academy. He later became a close family friend.

Brian Johnston – aka Johnners – much-loved BBC broadcaster, war hero and iconic *TMS* commentator. Together with Aggers he delivered one of BBC Radio's most memorable moments in what became known as the Legover Incident.

Mel Jones – Australia captain and leading batter who later captained Ebony at Surrey.

Mr Keating – Aatif's PE teacher at Preston Manor School, Wembley, who survived being struck (inadvertently) by Aatif's broken bat.

Peter Kelland – Sussex bowler who became Tuffers' first coach at Highgate School, north London.

David 'Bumble' Lloyd – England and Lancashire opener – Aggers' first victim in county cricket – now cricket broadcaster.

Simon Mann – sports journalist and *TMS* commentator.

Vic Marks – England and Somerset spin bowler, later *TMS* summariser and cricket writer.

Christopher Martin-Jenkins – BBC cricket correspondent and *TMS* commentator who famously invented his own swearwords.

Peter McConnell – Australian umpire who famously had a potty-mouthed exchange with Tuffers during Phil's 1990 England debut in Melbourne.

Henry Moeran – journalist and *TMS* commentator.

Don Mosey – cricket writer and *TMS* summariser

Adam Mountford – current *TMS* producer.

Dan Norcross – *TMS* commentator.

Eleanor Oldroyd – BBC Sport reporter and broadcaster.

Shilpa Patel – *TMS* assistant producer and fixer extraordinaire. Was often tasked with spotting celebrities in Test match crowds and persuading them to be interviewed.

Terry Rawlings – Aggers' first club captain at Ufford Park CC, Stamford.

Jack Robertson – England and Middlesex batter, later Middlesex youth coach. He persuaded the teenage Tuffers to switch from quick to spin bowling.

Eileen Ryder – Aggers' first cricket coach at Taverham Hall prep school near Norwich.

Andy Roberts – West Indies fast bowler with over 200 Test wickets who helped steer Aggers' early career at Leicestershire.

Andy Zaltzman – *TMS* scorer

Marlon Samuels – The batting partner who watched Carlos hit four sixes in the final over of the 2016 ICC Twenty20 championship to ensure West Indies beat England.

Allen Stanford – US fraudster whose 2008 sponsorship deal with the England and Wales Cricket Board ended in huge embarrassment for administrators.

Micky Stewart – Surrey batter and later England tour manager who played pivotal roles in both Tuffers' and Aggers' England careers,

Les Taylor – Quick bowler who came late to professional cricket with Leicestershire after working as a coal miner.

Mike Turner – chief executive at Leicestershire known simply as The Boss.

Frank 'Typhoon' Tyson – England bowler, among the fastest in cricket history, who took Aggers under his wing for a season in Australia.

Fred Titmus – Middlesex, Surrey and England all-rounder and briefly Aggers' coach at Surrey.

'Fiery' Fred Trueman – One of England's greatest fast bowlers, with over 300 Test wickets, and a *TMS* summariser.

Michael Vaughan – England's most successful Test captain who won 26 of his 51 Tests. A graceful opening bat with over 5700 Test runs, he became a *TMS* summariser.

Peter Willey – Leicestershire and England all-rounder who presided over 'Sweaty Betty' card games in the dressing room.

Bob Willis – England fast bowler with 325 Test wickets who inspired one of his country's greatest-ever Ashes victories at Headingley in 1981. Later endured the unenviable task of managing a Young England team, featuring Tuffers, on a Caribbean tour.

Don Wilson – Marylebone Cricket Club head coach who was instrumental in getting Tuffers a professional contract with Middlesex.

Jenny Wostrack – niece of West Indies cricketing legend Sir Frank Worrell. She played for Surrey, later worked on the club's community programme and discovered Ebony playing street cricket.

CHAPTER 1

EARLY STARTS

In which members of the *Test Match Special* team – Jonathan Agnew, Phil Tufnell, Alison Mitchell, Isa Guha, Ebony Rainford-Brent, Carlos Brathwaite and Aatif Nawaz – tell how they fell in love with cricket.

AGGERS

It doesn't take much for the greatest game on earth to lure kids in. A handed-down bat, a scuffed rubber ball, a stretch of garden or side street, your pal or a sibling – it's so often a sibling – and suddenly a dramatic Test match is being fought in the gathering gloom with enough disputed lbws, marginal run outs and dodgy catches to sustain days of outrage and argument. You won't forget the ball you managed to nip back to castle your brother or that towering six unfurled into the garden three doors down. You've discovered cricket and, once discovered, there's no turning back.

Which is how it was for pretty much every member of the *Test Match Special* team featured in this book. I'm going to bat first as I go back furthest, so I'm taking you to the late sixties, an idyllic farm on the south Lincolnshire border, a barn full of newly harvested wheat and barley, the rich, dulcet tones of *TMS* commentator John Arlott echoing out from a battered portable radio and, listening intently, the eight-year-old Jonathan Philip Agnew wondering if there would still be enough time for garden cricket with his dad before bed. There usually was.

Dad would spend hours teaching me a basic bowling action and how to grip a ball. He wanted me to be an off-spinner like him so in those early years that was my thing. Dad knocked around for a few local village clubs – Burghley Park was one – but although he was an enthusiastic cricketer it was hard for him to commit to games because he'd be tied up on the farm. He contented himself with

Test Match Special whenever it was on and that became the sound of summer for me. If I wasn't helping him I'd be inside watching entire Test matches on our black-and-white telly, curtains drawn, Mum interrupting with the occasional sandwich. And afterwards, my brother and I would dash out into the garden to copy what we'd seen.

Sometimes this would be taken to extremes. We noticed Ray Illingworth always bowled with his tongue poking out of the side of his mouth so we did that too when we were doing Ray's bowling style. He later became my first county captain, which now seems completely mad. In those years I just loved cricket. Lancashire was my team but I wrote off to all the counties asking for autographs and in those days they all sent autograph sheets back.

It was at prep school, though, that my cricketing talents began to flourish. I was dispatched aged eight to board at Taverham Hall, near Norwich, where my first proper cricket coach was Eileen Ryder, wife of one of our English teachers, Rowland Ryder, who later emerged as a well-respected cricket writer. The whole family was of sound cricketing stock and his father, confusingly also called Rowland, was secretary at Warwickshire CCC for 49 years. I later learned that the long-demolished Ryder Stand at Edgbaston was dedicated to Rowland Senior in recognition of his leadership during the club's formative years. He is said to have staged Edgbaston's first Test match in 1902 virtually single-handed.

Dear old Eileen always reminded me of the comedienne Joyce Grenfell, who played the hapless police sergeant Ruby Gates in the

St Trinian's films. She wore these long skirts, and was very old-fashioned in her mannerisms, but she had this shared love of cricket with her husband. She was my first coach when I arrived in the wilds of Norfolk and she took me under her wing. I will always remember the way she encouraged and supported me, and I know she thought I would be a decent cricketer one day. Years later, I managed to see her during a County Championship match at Edgbaston. We met outside the gates at the end of play – she must have phoned the dressing room or something – and I think it was pretty special for her. She was so kindly, incredibly enthusiastic, very matronly, very gentle and just perfect for both that sort of school and me.

NICE LINE

The essence of cricket

In addition to his teaching duties at Taverham School, Eileen Ryder's husband Rowland wrote three biographies, including that of a future president of the Marylebone Cricket Club, the senior Second World War British Army officer Lieutenant-General Sir Oliver Leese, KBE, CBE, DSO. Shortly before he died in 1996, Ryder published a series of essays titled *Cricket Calling* – a chapter of which, 'The Essence of Cricket', began: 'Cricket is not so much a game as an extension of being English: a gallimaufry of paradoxes, contradictions, frightening logic and sheer impossibilities, of gentle courtesy and rough violence.' A later essay told how Ryder once wrote to P. G. Wodehouse asking whether the writer's best-loved fictional character Jeeves was indeed named after the Warwickshire bowler Percy Jeeves. Wodehouse replied: 'Yes, you are quite right. It must have been in 1913 that I paid a visit to my parents in Cheltenham and went to see Warwickshire play Gloucestershire on the Cheltenham College ground. I suppose Jeeves's bowling must have impressed me, for I remembered him in 1916 when I was in New York and starting the Jeeves and Bertie saga, and it was just the name I wanted . . . (I remember admiring his action very much).'

To me, Taverham had elements of Arthur Ransome's children's adventure novel *Swallows and Amazons*, in which a group of children spends an idyllic summer camping, exploring and generally getting into mischief. And perhaps my love of pranks and practical jokes, which *TMS* colleagues have endured over the years, stems from those days. Boarding school isn't for everyone but it did me a lot of good. There were vast woodlands where you could go and build huts out of dead branches with your friends and then attack your neighbours' huts by setting fire to them – usually with boys still inside. Taverham was a beautiful old building on the River Wensum with two enormously long driveways. I well remember the sinking feeling as I was ferried back from holidays along these. But once you were there you got on with it and you were away. There was a lovely cricket field, a beautiful little pavilion and I was very lucky to have such a fortunate start in life.

My best mate was Chris Dockerty who went on to become an army major. Sadly he died aged 33 in that dreadful 1994 Chinook helicopter crash on the Mull of Kintyre during a flight from Northern Ireland to Scotland. I remember him as a very nervous, very homesick little boy yet he somehow rose to become this incredibly high-up figure in British military intelligence. He and I would improvise and play cricket anywhere – a tennis racket, table tennis bat – anything would do.

It was around this time, to the chagrin of my dad, that I started to feel spin bowling wasn't my true calling. For one thing, it had none of the glamour of fast bowling – storming in off a long run, terrorising batsmen with bouncers, flashing withering looks – which all seemed much more fun. I can even remember the precise moment I made the decision to switch; it was 1971, I was 11 years old and Dad had taken me to watch my beloved Lancashire playing Kent in the Gillette Cup final. It was a match we won comfortably by 24 runs with my hero Peter Lever posting figures of 11.2-4-24-3. I remember watching him bowl from the Nursery End. I had never seen anything like it and I told Dad: 'That's who I want to be.' Peter has since become a great friend – it's incredible how the wheel has gone full circle – and he's the loveliest, gentle man. He's the bowler I began to copy properly with his smooth, slingy action and long curving run-up. I modelled myself on him, although Dad was gutted.

To my surprise, I soon found I could bowl faster than anybody else of my age and quite substantially so. It was remarkable because I was so unbelievably thin. If you look at me, even in 1984 playing against the West Indies, I appear to be a walking bamboo cane. I was 12½ stone and 6ft 4in all the way through my career – there was nothing on me – and yet I could bowl a decent pace. I suppose it was coordination because it certainly wasn't brute strength.

There weren't that many opponents but we played each other home and away so we got plenty of games. There were school fixtures against Old Buckenham Hall and Gresham's, and our big local rival was Town Close, a Norwich prep school, which must have had one of the tiniest cricket grounds anywhere in the world. It felt like playing on a handkerchief. God only knows how I managed to fit in my run-up.

Once I became a fast bowler at Taverham, word soon got out among these other schools because I was the only player who could bowl bouncers at the age of 12. I had to give my wicketkeeper a code for when one was coming so I would reach the end of my mark and lift one foot behind me at a 45-degree angle, making it appear as though I was standing on one leg. Not very sophisticated but it did the job. The poor keeper would then have to retreat sharpish, hoping the batsman didn't clock what was happening, and take a ball zinging round his nose.

By the time I moved to senior school – Uppingham in Rutland – I was playing three years above my age group. It felt like quite a hard school environment – up on a hill, rather bleak and on winter nights you'd sleep with your clothes on. It also had a strong rugby-playing tradition and, although I loved watching rugby, I knew I would be a hopeless participant on the grounds of being far too feeble. I'd have been broken in half. The funny thing was that although I was something of an insignificant oik so far as the older lads were concerned, things changed rapidly when they saw how quickly I bowled.

During winter terms, I'd encounter the big bruisers from the 1st XV striding along the corridors, shoving me aside, and generally showing off to the girls who had just started being enrolled. But then those same lads would sidle up to me in the summer term, ahead of the annual staff v. pupils cricket match, urging me to make life uncomfortable for certain teachers. Conversations would go: 'Hey, Agnew, Dave Prince put me in detention last week. Sort him out, will you.' And I would bomb poor old Mr Prince, who taught

English and fancied himself as a bit of a batsman, and I'd be very popular for the summer term. But it would all revert to type in winter and I'd go back to being the lanky, weedy character who got pushed aside.

We played against several men's touring teams such as MCC and Leicester Gents, and I would certainly have been the quickest they'd seen. For schoolboys, with no real protection, or teachers who wandered out to the crease clad in a schoolmaster's mac, it would have been an interesting experience let's say. But every fast bowler is a bit of a bully and you need to have the competitive gene. I soon found out that quick bowling hurts. It's hard work and it's painful. You need to summon aggression and determination from within you. That's why, today, people are sometimes surprised to find the genial cricket commentator getting his dander up, but I'm still a fast bowler inside and I'll never lose that. So, if someone has a go at me, which has happened once or twice, I'm afraid it rises to the surface. That's how I got to be an international fast bowler. That said, most fast bowlers, when you get off the field, are thoroughly pleasant, friendly, intelligent people.

Uppingham was also where I had my first encounter with Brian Johnston, the man who years later would be my *TMS* partner-in-crime during the programme's most listened-to moment, when ball-by-ball commentary briefly bowed to unbridled, unstoppable hilarity. Johnners and I were on air together for what became known as 'The Legover', a radio event that *Radio Times* once called the 'funniest sporting blooper of all time' (see Chapter 12). But back in the mid-seventies, Johnners was a well-known celebrity outside cricket – he'd commentated for the BBC on various state occasions such as the Coronation in 1953 and the weddings of Princess Margaret and Princess Anne. He'd also served for ten years as the BBC's cricket correspondent and later became the permanent host of Radio 4's popular Sunday afternoon show *Down Your Way*, in which he would visit villages across the UK, interview the inhabitants and play their choice of music. So booking him as guest speaker gave Uppingham considerable kudos and he easily filled the 700-seat-capacity school hall.

I was still young, only in my second year. I'd heard him on *TMS* before and Dad said to make sure I went along to listen. I can recall exactly where I was sitting, gazing up at this tall, angular man standing at the lectern. He told all his usual stories but the one I always remember was his old chestnut about commentating for TV on the Queen Mother launching some ocean-going ship. As it slid down the ramp, the director suddenly switched to a shot of the Queen Mother. As Johnners tells it, he wasn't looking at the screen and was concentrating on the launch. So viewers saw the Queen Mother's face just as he said: 'There she is, the vast metal hulk of her', or words to that effect. It was typical Johnners and there's even a chance it might have been true.

TUFFERS

Around the same time that Aggers was politely listening to vaguely plausible Johnners stories at Uppingham, I would have been sat in the back of my dad's Ford Cortina, bound for a family summer holiday in Cornwall, desperately excited at the prospect of beach cricket and conscious that someone on the radio – probably John Arlott – was talking about a Test match. That's my first memory of *TMS*. I'd have been aged around six or seven, Dad would be driving and Mum would be handing out sandwiches in Tupperware. All I cared about was getting on to the beach with a bat and ball and having a knock with my brother and dad before bed.

Both my parents were sporty. We were a Middlesex and Arsenal FC household and that meant Denis Compton was a hero as he played for both. Mum was a decent net bowler and a good centre-half – she really would get stuck in – and so in winter our back garden would be a football pitch and in summer it would be a cricket ground. There was never much left of it. The roses never stood a chance.

I started off in all the top sets academically at Highgate School, which was a pretty posh public school. At the start, it was endless PE and sport with a bit of maths and English thrown in. We had some fantastic playing fields there but as I got older the sport got whittled away and the academic stuff got more important. I rebelled a bit against that, what with cricket and girls starting to look more fun.

Our cricket coach was the former Sussex bowler Peter Kelland. I used to come steaming in, left-arm fast in those days, and although it may be hard to believe I opened the batting for our school and was seen as a reliable covers fielder. In fact, I was the youngest pupil to win cricket colours and that was entirely for my batting. I do sometimes ask myself what on earth happened to Tufnell the batter. Whatever, years of playing with my brother in the back garden obviously got me a head start and Mr Kelland got me a youth trial at Middlesex. I was playing for the county Under 11s when I was still only 9.

Gordon Jenkins and Jack Robertson were my first coaches at Middlesex. Gordon was a stalwart of the Finchley indoor cricket school and I owe much of my success to him. He became a close family friend. Jack was a former England and Middlesex batter and an unforgettable coach. He would rock up, looking immaculate with his flicked-back, grey, Brylcreemed hair, white cravat, white dress shirt, flannels with turn-ups and whitened leather boots. It was an image that imbued confidence and suggested he knew what was what. It was Jack who first suggested I try spin bowling and I can remember word-for-word him saying: 'Yes, Phil, you're quick, nice action, but there are lots of quick bowlers around and not many left-arm spinners. Why not give it a go?'

I hadn't the faintest idea how to bowl spin so he showed me the grip, cut down my run and told me to 'open the door handle' as I released the ball. Crikey O'Reilly, my very first ball turned a bit, the kid at the stumps missed it and a little something sparked inside my head. My mum, always a canny observer, was sitting up on the viewing gallery, with her Coke and packet of crisps, when this happened. On the way home she said quietly: 'That looked good. Those batters didn't know what was happening. You should keep working on that.' And so I did.

ALISON

I was a sport-obsessed teenager for whom cricket was an essential part of family life. I grew up with an English dad, John, and an Australian mum, Kath, and although my brother Greg and I were both born and brought up in the UK, we travelled back to Australia every other Christmas to spend time with Mum's side of the family. There was a lot of family banter whenever an Ashes series was played and during the eighties and early nineties, Mum got the best of it. But it did gradually turn around. My dad and one of my Australian uncles bought a replica urn, which they would ceremoniously pass between them over a few beers whenever the Ashes changed hands.

Cricket was a huge part of our lives, as was Richie Benaud during those Aussie trips. We loved him and, inevitably, mimicked his commentary all the time. Then, much later, just before I obtained my journalism qualification and knowing I wanted to work in sports broadcasting, I managed to fix up a season with Channel 4 cricket for the 2001 Ashes series. I became Richie's tea- and coffee-maker, and in return got an amazing insight into the art of commentary and the discipline of broadcasting. Just being able to watch and observe a man whose voice was ingrained into my childhood – that was very special.

I was sports mad as a kid – hockey, netball and tennis, which were on offer at school – but this was a time when cricket wasn't usually offered to girls and aside from playing against my brother I hardly featured in competitive cricket matches. I spent loads of time down at the Embankment Club in Wellingborough, Northamptonshire, which is where my dad played, and I inherited my love of the game from him and my brother. Mum was involved too, and I'd help out with the scoring and the teas and then play on the boundary with the other kids, having a brilliant time. Cricket studs clattering on concrete steps is such an evocative sound for me because it conjures up those summer days as men would go in and out to bat.

I did fill in a couple of times for my brother's club side and he actually taught me a pretty good forward defensive stroke (although I'm more of a fan of a good swipe now!). I never bowled but I got to bat once. I had to use whatever kit was lying around and by then he and his team-mates would have been 15 or 16, a couple of years older than me, and the pads were massive. I ended up batting with one of his mates who had gone through a growth spurt and took one stride for my three. So he'd already completed a second run while I was still floundering halfway down the pitch in these ridiculous pads trying to come back for two. It wasn't a lengthy partnership.

I never pushed to pursue playing cricket myself. I was happy playing with my brother and cousins in the garden and enjoying my hockey and netball. I never questioned why girls weren't offered the chance to play cricket or football at my school. Thankfully there's been a generational shift and girls' cricket is now much easier to find in clubs and schools, and of course now feeds into professionalism. There are role models visible on television. We now even hear of girls who have got into cricket because an older *sister* has played.

ISA

My cricketing apprenticeship was particularly unforgiving because
it revolved around my elder brother Kaush needing batting practice
and requiring someone to bowl at him. Who better than his little
sister? It was the classic sibling story. Kaush was seven years older
than me and would usually get me out first or second ball,
whereupon I would have to bowl at him for the rest of the evening.
It hardened me up, though, and at least I got used to bowling
uphill into the wind as our garden sloped upwards. It was long and
thin – pretty much cricket-pitch shape – and we would be forever
nagging Dad to cut the grass. He was very supportive although less
so when the ball smashed a window.

I learned a lot just by watching my brother play. He was very wristy
and by the age of 15 had a good technique. He went to the Royal
Grammar School in High Wycombe, renowned for its cricket
prowess, so I just tried to copy his batting. As for bowling, I just had
a go and nobody told me I was doing anything wrong. I then got
into a boys' colts team at High Wycombe and there were a couple of
guys there who spent a lot of time coaching me. One was Kelly
Rogers, originally from the Caribbean, and the other was Bob Lester
with whom Dad set up a girls' team. My parents didn't see any
problem with a girl playing in a boys' team and so no-one else did
either. As for the boys, the only thing they cared about was not
getting bowled by a girl.

At first, my bowling action felt strange and unlike anything my fellow players were doing. In my delivery stride I would jump with my right foot but wouldn't cross my legs over before it landed again, by which time my arm was already over. The rhythm wasn't there. I'd look at other bowlers and think: 'Why can't I do that? I'm not doing it right.' I'd tried and failed to sort out the problem in the nets but then suddenly, in the middle of a game, it just clicked. From that point on, I was fine. I was always a visual learner, I had to see things rather than feel them.

My love of cricket stems from my dad Barun and my mum Rama, who were both massive fans. It was in their genes. When Dad was growing up in Kolkata he would go to Eden Gardens to watch cricket. And if he couldn't get in he'd climb up the outside of the stands to get a decent view. He saw a few classic Test matches like that. Mum was really proud of my progress as a cricketer – she was a huge influence on me but she never piled on the pressure. For her, it was all about letting us do what we wanted to do.

They both played a big role in my development as a player; Dad would drive me all over the country – cricket in the summer; badminton in winter – while Mum would take me to matches in the evenings. They even used to come on England tours with me. Parental support is vital, which is why it's even more of an achievement when people are able to excel in sport without family help.

EBONY

I was spotted as a potential future professional by the late Jenny
Wostrack, a niece of the great West Indian all-rounder Sir Frank
Worrell. She played for Surrey and organised a lot of their
community cricket. She saw me playing on some inner-city street
one day, got me in at Surrey, drove me everywhere, found me
scholarships and generally helped my mum juggle everything. Mum
encouraged and supported me but without Jenny I would never
have played professional cricket.

NICE LINE
Sir Frank Worrell

Sir Frank Mortimer Maglinne Worrell was one of the greatest Caribbean cricketers ever to take the field. During the 1940s, an era in which West Indies Test teams were white-dominated, his stylish batting and heavy run-scoring forced the selectors to take note. After making his debut in 1948, he was appointed captain two years later – the first black cricketer to lead the Windies for an entire series – and not only quashed stubborn cliques within the team but turned his players into world-beaters. Gradually, with humour and subtlety, he broke down the old inter-island rivalries to make the West Indies more than the sum of their parts.

His first series in Australia, pitting him against revered opposing captain Richie Benaud, was noteworthy for producing the first tie in the history of Test cricket. On the final day of the match at Brisbane, and with Australia on 227 for 7 needing only six runs off the last (then eight-ball) over for victory, an astonishing series of deliveries took place. These included a leg bye, a bye, a caught-behind, a dropped catch and two run outs. At the time of writing there has been only one other tie, in 1986 between Australia and India.

The Windies tourists lost the 1960–1 series 2–1 but could easily have won it and, in terms of winning the hearts and minds of the Australian public, Worrell certainly did win. His side were treated to an open-top bus procession through the streets of Melbourne on their departure as tens of thousands of cheering fans paid tribute to their emergence as a world cricketing power.

CARLOS

I can't remember a time when I *wasn't* playing cricket. My dad
Chesterfield reckons that after a long day at work I used to force
him to throw balls for me. I was apparently only three at the time
and I would drive them into the wall behind him. He claims I drove
the ball better then than I do now. I guess cricket is in my blood
because my cousin Jonathan Carter has also played for the West
Indies ODI team and featured in the 2015 World Cup.

I played street cricket almost every day. We'd use a fairly narrow road
and the rules were that if you struck the ball so that it hit a wall or
house either side then you were out. That meant you had to try and
play the ball along the ground. Bowlers would bowl short, not just to
try and take your head off, but also in the hope you would pull or cut
straight on to a house. We got into trouble all the time because,
obviously, the neighbours weren't always happy and that meant the
ball got confiscated.

And there was another street cricket rule that was unfortunately in
direct conflict with one of my mum Joycelyn's rules. She always
insisted that before I went out to play in the evening I had to finish
my homework. But street cricket rules said that if you were the not-
out batsman at the end of play then you got to bat first the
following evening. And one particular day that was me. I got home
late from school but mum still insisted I should have a shower and
do my homework first, which meant I would definitely miss my
chance. So I hatched a plan which involved me turning on the

shower and dashing out for a quick bat before coming back to do my homework. But it was more than a quick bat, and when I got home I'd turned the house into a steam room with water everywhere. Mum did not see the funny side.

Growing up, my biggest cricketing mentor was Roddy Estwick, my PE teacher at Combermere Secondary School, Barbados. He was a great cricket coach and something of a father figure to us teenagers at an age when a lot of vices are thrown at you. Roddy was instrumental in keeping us on the straight and narrow. He went on to play first-class cricket for Barbados and later became regional assistant coach to the West Indies team. He was also Rihanna's gym teacher. A big man with a big heart, for sure.

AATIF

I fell in love with cricket aged about six or seven after being taken to watch the Pakistan touring team. I thought they were so cool. It could have been the West Indies, Sri Lanka or anyone but it happened to be Pakistan, and I bonded with them in the same way I bonded with Arsenal after they won the Coca-Cola Cup. I've lived to regret both decisions but there's no going back now. I loved Pakistan as a cricket team before I even realised it was a country. People often ask me why I support them and it's nothing to do with geographical location or the fact my parents were born there.

Growing up, it certainly wasn't all plain sailing out in the middle. During one innings for my school team, Preston Manor in Wembley, I was nearing the end of a decent captain's knock against one of our local rivals. I was middling everything, sixes, fours, the lot, and we needed only ten to win when I attempted an extravagant pull shot. My bat broke at the splice. I held on to the handle but the business end went spiralling wildly to square leg where it smacked our PE teacher square in the face. What are the chances? It could have been nasty but wasn't, which is just as well because players and teachers on both sides were laughing till it hurt. I avoided him for the rest of the day and skipped the team bus home even though the three-mile walk with a kit bag wasn't fun. For the next match, I sat in on the team talk with my cap over my eyes, trying to avoid looking at him. I was doing GCSE PE and convinced myself I'd be a nailed-on fail. Fortunately, he didn't hold a grudge. But I never apologised so, if you're reading this, Mr Keating, I am really very sorry.

TOP LIST

Biggest influence as a cricketer

AGGERS Peter Willey. He hardened me up in the early 1980s when he was stand-in captain for David Gower and I suspect I would not have played for England without him.

TUFFERS Probably my fellow spinner at Middlesex, John Emburey. He taught me you couldn't just bowl and hope for the best. You had to 'think' batters out.

ISA Darren Gough. The way he played the game, his charisma, the way he always tried to make something happen, be it with the bat or the ball, to influence a game. I tried to emulate that in my cricket.

EBONY The late Jenny Wostrack whose uncle was the iconic West Indian all-rounder Sir Frank Worrell. Jenny played for Surrey and was way ahead of her time in making the women's game more accessible. She spotted me playing cricket in the streets, got me in at Surrey, drove me everywhere and generally helped my mum.

CARLOS Roddy Estwick, my former PE teacher at Combermere Secondary School in Barbados. A great coach, father figure and defender of us teenage boys. He also taught Rihanna.

AATIF Always a tough choice between Wasim Akram and Waqar Younis. I had posters of them both on my bedroom wall growing up – slightly odd because batting is my thing.

CHAPTER 2

OFF TO A CLUB

In which Tuffers enjoys a rum do and Aggers
meets a one-eyed bowling partner.

TUFFERS

If you're part of a cricket club you'll know it's as much a way of life as it is a sporting experience. Whether it be pub side, village or city team or scratch gathering in the park, grassroots cricket is the heartbeat of the modern game. Aside from which, the transition from school to club is often an amazing release for young cricketers. In the right environment, there's a freedom to try new things, make mistakes, get advice (though not too much), laugh about shared misfortune, meet extraordinary characters, form lifelong friendships and take the first steps towards making it as a pro. Mind you, in my own case, those steps were shaky. Let's be honest, I nearly blew it.

It had all started so well with selection for Middlesex Under 11s while I was still only nine years old. Once my coach, Jack Robertson, persuaded me to switch from fast bowling to spin, it was a life-changing moment and set me on the path to a professional career. But it was not always a clear path and I think it's fair to say I wandered off many times. There seems little point in revisiting the detail of what we might call my rebel teenage years but a heavily abridged version might read: girls, booze, cigarettes and punk rock, more girls, substances (various), more girls, fights, expulsion from Highgate School, parties, motorbikes and, finally, departure from Southgate Comprehensive with an O level in Art. It wasn't the most compelling CV to wave in the face of a prospective employer and I make no excuses. The responsibility was all mine. But had I not lost my mum – a strong, charismatic, powerful woman – to leukaemia at that time, things might have turned out rather differently.

With few obvious employment opportunities beckoning, I went to work for my dad as a trainee silversmith, a job which at least gave me some breathing space. He then conjured up a plan to rekindle my interest in cricket by putting me back in touch with Finchley CC, where I'd occasionally played as a schoolboy. I was given a game for Finchley Fifths on a dodgy park pitch alongside rotund team-mates who had, hopefully, seen better days. I spent one mind-numbingly dull afternoon fielding on the boundary as those team-mates served up a veritable feast of buffet bowling for the batters to help themselves. They had racked up around 300 for 2 before I was eventually given two, pointless, overs.

In fairness, although Finchley was a good and successful club, it didn't have much of a youth set-up. I wouldn't have been able to get into the 1st XI because they had a spinner who'd been there 30 years. After that awful match, Dad went straight home and penned a letter to the club in which he essentially said he wasn't going to have his son playing for a side whose bowling attack was decided on the basis of heaviest bowls first. He then dispatched me to try my luck at Southgate CC but, again, it wasn't the greatest carrot to dangle. I was 16 and weekdays I'd be sitting at my dad's hammering stall – 386 St John's Street – silversmithing for him all day long. So weekends and a bit of free time were important. I'd got my motorbike and there was the prospect of hanging around the park with a few girlfriends. Cricket was slipping away until, as sometimes happens in life, the outlook changed with extraordinary speed. In my case, it was quite literally a case of bowling the right ball at the right time.

Dad had persuaded me to attend a coaches' training session with Les Lenham, the former Sussex player, who was running a batting tutorial. Loads of boys I knew were there – we were basically guinea pigs to whom trainee coaches were expected to impart cricket skills. Len started demonstrating the on-drive and asked me to bowl just short of a length on leg stump. To which I sent down this beautiful, flighted delivery, which turned sharply and beat his outside edge. He was pretty impressed, people took notice and not long afterwards Gordon Jenkins, my old Middlesex Under 11s coach, got me back into the club game with MCC Young Cricketers. Suddenly I was in the system, under the eyes of good coaches, having a great time with my MCC mates and getting paid by Dad to boot. And then I got picked up by Middlesex.

My first few months at the Middlesex youth academy went like a dream. Although still almost two years away from my County Championship debut, I was picked for the 1984–5 Young England side to tour the West Indies. The late England fast bowler Bob Willis, a National Treasure following his destruction of Australia at Headingley three years earlier, was appointed manager for that trip and whatever they paid him it couldn't have been enough. We arrived at this little guesthouse called Harbour Lights, right on the beach in Barbados, the first time any of us had been anywhere exotic. We were all togged up in our grey trousers, light-blue shirts and Young England blazers, but as soon as the cases were unloaded we sprinted for the beach, kicked off our shoes and socks and went for a paddle. Bob had given us the afternoon off to acclimatise and there was to be a nets session the following morning.

Someone found a bottle of Cockspur rum, which was shared around, and then it was back to the hotel to get changed, all 16 of us, very excited, very Cockspurred, and out we went into the Barbados night. We came staggering back at 3 a.m. having had our first experience of reggae and rum punch to find Bob Willis sat in the lobby with a clipboard ticking off names saying: 'You're fired . . . you're fired . . .' In fact, he restricted himself to an omni-bollocking, threats to call our parents, threats to send us home, a standard reminder about representing our country and a curfew order for the rest of the tour. We were all a bit sheepish for three days but the curfew soon got forgotten, largely because we discovered the back door of the guesthouse. Years later, I was still greeting Bob as 'The Manager', although it wasn't a role that sat naturally with him. He liked a bit of fun himself and babysitting a load of 16- and 17-year-olds on their first outing to the Caribbean was not it.

NICE LINE

The Bob Willis Ashes Show, Headingley, 1981

'Legend' is a way-overused word in cricket. You can argue it should be reserved only for consistent greatness over many years. Perhaps only for the record-breakers and the innovators, the players who mesmerised with their strokeplay or bowling prowess. And while these are all fair-enough legend categories, they fade alongside those who, against all odds and logic, and through sheer force of will, turn a single match from hopelessly lost to gloriously won. For England supporters, the name of Robert George Dylan Willis is high on that elite and hallowed list. Especially as he did it to the Aussies.

First, it has to be said that Willis should never have been in a position to work his fast-bowling magic at Headingley that Tuesday afternoon in July 1981. Winning the toss, Australia had batted first, posted 401, bowled England out for 174 and enforced the follow-on. Ian Botham's magnificently pugnacious 149 not out in the second innings allowed some semblance of a target to be set for the tourists but it was a mere 130. On the morning of the final day, Botham got an early wicket but Willis looked nothing special in his first spell. And England's other quick bowler, Graham Dilley, bowling with the wind, was taken off by skipper Mike Brearley after just two overs. Soon the target was down to a paltry 74 with nine wickets standing.

Brearley now played his final card. Thirty minutes before lunch he brought the tall, gangly, 32-year-old Willis back into the attack – only this time from the Kirkstall Lane end from where he could catch the wind. Almost immediately it became clear that England had a new Bob. A much faster and decidedly scary Bob. At 56 for 1 he got a ball to lift viciously at Trevor Chappell who haplessly ballooned it to wicketkeeper Bob Taylor. Moments later, Willis had both Kim Hughes and Graham Yallop out for ducks but, still, hopes of an England victory looked delusional. Australia would surely regroup and knock off the 72 they needed – especially with the stubborn opener John Dyson still at the crease. Brearley's instruction to Willis over the Headingley lunch spread was simple: 'Bowl your fastest and keep digging it in.'

And he did. Once Chris Old had bowled Allan Border, the scene was set for the Bob Willis Show. Wide-eyed, arms pumping, mop of hair flying, he bowled and looked like a man possessed. He got Dyson with the score on 68, Rod Marsh on 74 (a brilliant Dilley catch on the boundary) and Geoff Lawson on 75. The ground was in uproar and Willis fed off it. And yet Australian teams are nothing if not proud and defiant. Ray Bright and Dennis Lillee counterattacked, adding 35 in four overs, until Willis dismissed Lillee and, in a memorable denouement, uprooted Bright's middle stump with a yorker before wheeling away, arms aloft, to send Headingley into raptures. Australia had lost by 18 runs and yet Willis's extraordinary figures of 15.1-3-43-8 told only half the story. Had Australia won that 3rd Test they would have been 2–0 up in the series with just three to play. As it was, mentally scarred by Willis and a re-energised Botham, they lost the next two Test matches and ended 3–1 down.

AGGERS

During the school summer holidays I played for Ufford Park, near Stamford, the closest village club to our family's Lincolnshire farm. It's a beautiful little ground – basically a treelined cow field – and I was gleefully welcomed into the fold as a raw, young speed merchant who would hopefully put the fear of God into local rivals. Dad took me down there to introduce me to the captain, a chap called Terry Rawlings, and I was sort of handed over to Terry with the unsaid implication: 'Here's the lad – see what you think.'

I must have been about 13 or 14 at the time so a season in men's cricket was both a bit daunting and, I told myself, valuable experience. It certainly proved an experience. At least once in every game the cry would go up, 'The cows are coming,' and everyone had to dash off to the neighbouring cow field where the cars were parked while play was suspended. Cows would slobber over the windscreens and bite off the aerials so there was a sense of urgency. For some of our fielders, it was the fastest they ever moved.

There were great characters such as my opening bowling partner Baggy Bagshaw, who unfortunately had only one eye. The other was glass. I never had the temerity to enquire what had happened but, from a strictly cricketing viewpoint, it didn't much matter. Despite his visual impairment, Baggy was metronomically accurate. He had no real pace but would land every delivery on a length, which made him extremely difficult to hit. I tried to bowl like him but usually failed because I was too young and wild.

As the years went by, I got quicker but I wasn't available for Ufford so often. On the occasions I *could* play, Terry, who essentially did everything and was the best batsman, would head off to the nearest sports shop and splurge hard-earned club funds on a new ball especially for me. Such a purchase was an incredibly rare event and expectations were consequently high. Unfortunately, Terry would soon be tearing his hair out from his position at gully as I wasted the ball on a series of hooping wides. No-one thought it was funny.

The rivalry between the villages was amazing. There were grudges that had been held 30 years, and Terry wanted to make the most of me, theoretically his most potent weapon, to settle a few. Rather too often, I let him down and he graciously resigned himself to this as the inevitable by-product of youth.

For me, playing at Ufford provided a grounding for which I will always be grateful. Doing the sometimes rather pompous job I do, I occasionally need to look back and remind myself how village cricket shaped me both as a player and later as a sports journalist.

By my mid-teens, it was clear I had a bit of promise so Dad decided it was time for a step up in terms of coaching. During the 1970s, the Alf Gover cricket school at Wandsworth, southwest London, was considered the best in the country for developing potential county players and Alf came with an impressive CV. In the modern game, he still holds the record for most number of wickets taken by a fast bowler in an English season – 201 in 1937. As a Surrey stalwart he was also particularly well connected.

So, for my sixteenth birthday present, Dad and I drove down to Alf's coaching school. I don't know what we were expecting but we found it in the most incongruous setting above a petrol station – the entrance was an anonymous door straight off the street. You walked through this gloomy changing room reeking of stale sweat and then out into a long nets hall with low ceilings and gaslights. There were some lovely coaches, including the Australian wrist-spinner John McMahon, and even at this stage I think Dad was hoping I might be seduced by spin. Then there was Alf himself, a great character who would hold court in his England kit, set off with a stylish neckerchief, call everyone 'old boy' and recount anecdotes from his playing career at every opportunity.

One of his favourites came from a winter tour of India – amazingly he was capped only four times – and related to a game upcountry where dysentery had gone through the camp. On the opening morning Alf was apparently still fit so they threw him the ball for the first over. He began his great long run and came tearing in only to be gripped halfway through by these terrible stomach cramps. So he raced past the umpire, past the batsman on strike, through the slips and straight for the dressing room. He told that story many times, although the punchline was always the same. He lost the race by two yards.

NICE LINE
Alf Gover

During the 1930s, Alf Gover's record for Surrey, bowling mainly on placid, batter-friendly Oval pitches, was outstanding. In 1933, his first year as a regular 1st XI player, he took 98 County Championship wickets and then bagged 171 in the unusually wet 1936 season when pitches were unsuited to pace. In 1937 – dubbed Gover's Golden Summer – he posted the magic figure of 201 wickets in a single season, a performance that earned him an England call-up for the 1937 winter tour to India.

Perhaps one reason Gover was such an effective coach lay in the technical difficulties he himself suffered during his playing days. He was bedevilled by overstepping the crease in his delivery stride and eventually sought help at a cricket school run by the former England wicketkeeper Herbert Strudwick. Gover later cited Strudwick and Surrey bowler William 'Razor' Smith as the key coaches who, through hours of painstaking practice, helped him iron out his run.

Gover recognised my potential straightaway and introduced me to Surrey's youth team manager, the former England wicketkeeper Arthur McIntyre. This turned out to be both a curse and a blessing. On the one hand, I loved the challenge of playing at a high level. But I hated the hierarchical, often demeaning, culture that accompanied it. I had two summer holidays at the Oval, aged 16 and 17, playing youth and 2nd XI cricket, and in many ways it was an amazing time. Dad had no real knowledge of London – he was a Lincolnshire farmer; he had no contacts – but he somehow found a B&B run by a Mrs Bushell in Morden. She was a kindly old woman and it was a short walk to Morden Underground, which took me straight along the Northern Line to the Oval. Leaving a young country lad alone in the big city was an agonising decision for Mum and Dad but they thought this arrangement was the best they could do and I suppose they were right.

Even so, I found it hard. Apart from cricket, I had nothing. I didn't know anybody and I hated it at the Oval. It was a very old-fashioned, bullying kind of atmosphere in which the young lads were treated like dirt. We were shouted at all the time. The senior pros were clinging to their places and there was this really unhealthy structure. No-one made any effort to make me feel welcome and I was pretty miserable. I now realise it had been like that a long time at Surrey and still was up until around 2009, when Alec Stewart was appointed coach and mentoring consultant and sorted it out a bit.

The worst example of this execrable coaching environment came in the form of blatant racism by Surrey's coach, the England bowling 'legend' Fred Titmus. It was July 1977; I was in my second summer at Surrey and still very much on trial. There had been a significant change to the set-up at Surrey in that Titmus had been brought in as head coach. I had never met him before and he would now be the man who would decide whether or not I had a future as a professional cricketer. We were playing in a Surrey 2nd XI game against Hampshire at Guildford Cricket Club when, during a break in proceedings, Titmus turned on our captain – again a man I did not know – the Guyanese wicketkeeper Lonsdale Skinner. The language was completely unacceptable and I told Titmus so. Years later, Lonsdale recalled the event and I think he appreciated me taking a stand. What happened was outrageous and, at that point, I hated the place and got out. I'm proud that I stood up for Lonsdale, who is the gentlest, loveliest man. It means a lot that he's remembered it.

NICE LINE

Aggers calls out his coach

In an interview with the *Guardian*, Lonsdale Skinner recalled the
moment a teenage Agnew stood up for him as Surrey coach Fred
Titmus spouted appalling racist language. 'He was calling me
black bastard and that kind of stuff,' said Skinner. 'Agnew jumped
up and said: "You shouldn't be doing this, it's not on." He was
playing for Surrey twos, down on trial. Titmus was carrying on in
front of everybody and Agnew said: "No, no, this is not acceptable."
He was the only one who stood up.' Skinner clearly appreciated the
support and later gave young Aggers some frank advice, seasoned
wicketkeeper to raw fast bowler. 'He was genuinely quick in those
days,' Skinner recalled. 'I used to tell him: "Don't pitch it up to these
public schoolboys, put it across their ears." '

Although I left Surrey with unhappy memories, I'd at least proved to myself that I was good enough to play professionally. I'd done the England Schools route and was in the Surrey 2nd XI at 16 or 17, which in those days was very young. So I was doing all right. When Dad sent me to the Oval, I felt it was somehow him giving me his blessing to be a pro-cricketer. Ten years at boarding school had been a big financial commitment for him; here was someone who worked every hour God sent on a modest 200-acre arable farm. There was no way our family could have made a living out of that alone so Dad relied on free-range turkeys and a farm shop to push up income. I would come back from months at boarding school and go straight into the plucking shed – I didn't actually kill the birds – and then on to handle Christmas sales. The public would come streaming up, including England and Northants batsman David Steele, which made Dad very pleased; he always gave him a free one. But even after the Oval, I don't think Dad was convinced I could make cricket a career.

Around this time, the late seventies, universities were tapping up players to ensure they could turn out decent teams. I had an offer from Durham to do European Studies, which I suspect involved very little apart from playing cricket for them and getting rewarded with a degree to provide security outside cricket. But I didn't fancy it. I also declined Dad's idea of fixing me up a job in Germany. I think he just sort of surrendered after that.

After the Titmus episode, I returned to Uppingham School where I informed my cricket coach, the former Leicestershire batsman and captain Maurice Hallam, that if that was professional cricket I didn't want any part of it. Hallam reassured me that it wasn't all like that and promised to make a few calls to his former county side. As a result Mike Turner, the chief executive of Leicestershire, came over to Uppingham three times in 1978 to watch me bowl. It rained on every occasion and he never saw me in action. But he signed me anyway because Maurice told him to.

Within weeks I found myself ensconced in digs provided by Leicestershire. It was a B&B on Grace Road and my fellow residents were fast bowlers Ken Shuttleworth, Ken Higgs and Alan Ward. The place was run by a Yugoslavian proprietor called Radi and he insisted that 'Mr Higg', as he called him, always had a table to himself because he was senior among us. We had to sit separately on our own little table like three naughty boys. But I was well set up; they taught me a lot, and I'm still very good friends with Ken Shuttleworth. It was such an exciting time because, just three weeks after signing, the expanding first-team injury list meant I was thrown straight into a County Championship game. And who should be the first team I faced but Lancashire, the county side I'd supported all my life – my absolute heroes.

AATIF

My dad lived and breathed cricket so you can imagine his enthusiasm once I started playing for clubs in the early 1990s. When I scored my first century in an adult game as a 13-year-old playing for South Hampstead against Millfields it made headlines in the local newspaper. My dad bought 50 copies to show people and still to this day keeps one in his car. Embarrassing or what? It matters more to him than my comedy awards, my BBC Three show or pretty much anything else I've done. I also played at Under 13 level for Middlesex and got into the Under 16 squad, unfortunately without playing a game.

Playing league cricket for a club can be a bit edgy and there has been the odd time I've chucked my toys out of the pram. I remember one particular game playing for Ruislip Victoria in the Berkshire Cricket League when we'd bowled in the rain, the opposition had posted 300-plus and I got out early for 7. As is the way in club cricket, I was quickly turned around and sent back out to do an umpiring shift. We had no chance of winning but our batters were inching their way to 175 to try and get a bonus point.

This is obviously irritating for a bowling side in a winning position and the opposition's 16-year-old bowler was flouncing around, rolling his eyes and offering to give us the point because it was so boring. I lost it and rounded on him: 'Shut up, stop whingeing and bowl. We bowled at you in the wet. We didn't complain, so f***ing bowl at us.' He did shut up and his captain apologised.

But I was dropped for the return fixture. I still play for a club and, because my name is on the back of my shirt, I get identified as 'that guy on *TMS*'. This presents two problems. Firstly, players think I must be really good. And secondly, they really want my scalp.

EBONY

I made my Surrey senior debut as a 15-year-old. I was desperate to impress but I have a short attention span and, although I'd been told to stay in the ring of fielders, I drifted ever closer to the stumps. I'd forgotten there was a safety rule on fielding distances. Inside the first 30 minutes, someone nailed a ball, I headbutted it, my temple sprouted a huge egg and I spent the rest of the day in hospital being checked for concussion.

I owe a lot to Mel Jones, the Australian batter, who was an idol of mine and who later captained me at Surrey. She was so strict but she made me understand that you had to take professional sport seriously. She would drill us until we threw up, then lead us in partying hard. She's a great friend now.

ISA

My worst moment on a cricket pitch was my very first TV game at
Durham as a 17-year-old playing for England. I was into my second
spell, the camera was on me and just as I got into my delivery stride
I suddenly disappeared from shot. On screen, the camera
was desperately panning left and right to try and find me but I
was actually on the floor having slipped on the side of my boot.
I was so embarrassed I got up in one quick motion as though it was
all planned. The clip got played on TV for weeks, including once in
front of Freddie Flintoff, who laughed uncontrollably. Freddie was
a hero of mine, which then made me feel even worse.

CARLOS

As kids, we'd play on the street and then the local club circuit in
Barbados. Dad played and I'd always tag along with him so I spent
weekends at one of his two clubs, Dover and Lodge Road. He was a
diminutive batter who enjoyed short bowling – he loved to cut and
pull – and he was a specialist short leg who still holds a fielding
record on Barbados after taking seven catches in a single day. His
nickname was MacGyver, taken from the US TV series of the same
name featuring the adventures of a resourceful secret agent. This
was supposedly because he could get himself out of sticky situations
when the ball was smashed his way. And because he always managed
to make things happen for his team.

TOP LIST

Best cricketing moment

AGGERS Getting Viv Richards lbw on my debut in the 1984 West Indies Test.

TUFFERS January 1992, 1st Test, Christchurch, New Zealand. We'd rattled up 580 for 9 in our first innings and I then took four of New Zealand's top five wickets to reduce them to 312. Graham Gooch enforced the follow-on but the game was set for a draw until I took 7–47 in the Black Caps' second innings to help us win by an innings and four runs.

ISA Winning the World Cup in 2009. There were seven years of emotion built into that. I'd come into the England team in 2002 and in 2005 we went to the South Africa World Cup thinking we were better than we were and got a salutary lesson from Australia, who knocked us out in the semi-finals. So, to make that journey on to 2009, to win with people you'd got so close to, who were almost family, it was bond-for-life stuff.

I was full of nerves. It wasn't my best game with the ball – 1–24 off five overs – and although we were cruising towards New Zealand's total of 166, wickets suddenly started tumbling. Charlotte Edwards went, Beth Morgan was run out and a bit of panic set in. Huge credit was due to Nicky Shaw, who didn't even know she was playing until the morning of the game. She'd already taken four wickets and now she steadied things in a partnership with Holly Colvin. By then,

I was camped out in the dressing room strapping my pads on and that's never a good sign. All I could think was, 'Please don't make me bat,' but they hit the winning runs and the relief was incredible.

The seeds were sown in 2005. We'd lost to Australia in the World Cup but in England later that same year we beat them for the first time in ten years in a one-day international. Laura Newton and Clare Taylor were smashing Cathryn Fitzpatrick back over her head for four, and we were looking at each other in astonishment. Cathryn was the best bowler in the world; here she was conceding 61 runs from ten overs. Nobody had done this before. We got past 200, which we'd never managed, and then defended it against Australia. It was a massive moment in our careers. We huddled together on the pitch and in that moment knew we could beat anybody.

EBONY Winning the 2009 World Cup in Sydney. For years we'd been losing and getting hammered but we gradually turned it around as a team and won that tournament, something we'd all dreamed of.

CARLOS Beating England in the Twenty20 World Cup final in front of 66,000 people at Eden Gardens, India. It wasn't just those four sixes which won us the match in the last over. It was how much that win meant to people in the West Indies and the fact that we won when still needing 19 runs from six balls. To do that on the huge stage that is Eden Gardens was an amazing feeling. I was on strike for that last over but I didn't go out thinking I was going to hit sixes. I just played the balls on their merit. Plus, my partner Marlon Samuels had told me to make sure I got the ball in the air – this would give us time to cross and get him on strike in the event that I got myself out caught.

TOP LIST
Worst cricketing moment

AGGERS Treading on a grass-coloured tennis ball while fielding at Grace Road and having to be taken from the field in the groundsman's wheelbarrow.

TUFFERS New Year's Day 1991, a World Series one-dayer against Australia. I just had to catch a return throw to break the stumps and run out Steve Waugh, but the ball bounced off my hands. I could have retrieved it and *walked* back to break the stumps: Steve had already given up. But instead I decided to throw, missed, and he got home. Around 65,000 Aussies absolutely loved it. They kept showing my shame on the big screen.

ISA Falling over in my delivery stride during my first TV game at Durham as a 17-year-old. I was so embarrassed I jumped up as though I meant to do it – which just made it look worse. The clip got played on TV for weeks.

EBONY My Surrey senior debut. I was 15, desperate to impress but kept drifting closer and closer to the batter despite my captain's instructions. A batter smashed the ball at me, I headbutted it, got a bump the size of an egg and spent the rest of the day in hospital.

CARLOS I've got at least two. I've always had stick for how slowly I run between the wickets and this was embarrassingly clear when, during a 2018 World Cup qualifier in Zimbabwe, Rovman Powell called me for a quick single and then sent me back. The highlights showed me taking the best part of a day to turn around before failing to save my wicket. There was an image of me going around under the heading: 'No U-turns for Carlos'. Then there was the 2019 World Cup at Old Trafford, West Indies against New Zealand. It was the second delivery of the day – I couldn't have been any fresher because the first had resulted in a wicket – and when the ball got pushed through mid-on I gave chase. But I never seemed to be getting any closer. In the end, I dived full length, clawed at the ball, came up with a handful of air, hit my head on the boundary rope and looked round to see the ball hadn't even reached the boundary. Good comedy value for the supporters, and for the next two overs the ball followed me everywhere. Although we lost, the day ended rather better, though, because I scored a century.

ALISON As a teenager I once got drafted in to play for my elder brother's club. I had to borrow his pads, which were enormous on me, and was left floundering between the wickets as my batting partner managed three strides for every one of mine. It wasn't a lengthy partnership.

AATIF In a school game, my bat broke at the splice as I attempted a pull shot. Our PE teacher was fielding at square leg and it smashed him in the face. I was convinced he would fail me at GCSE PE but fortunately he didn't hold a grudge.

CHAPTER 3

COUNTY SET – SEVENTIES AND EIGHTIES

In which Aggers suffers the most humiliating
entry in the history of first-class cricket, gives
himself out to escape Malcolm Marshall
and gets sledged for 'wobbling cheeks'.

AGGERS

As the veteran among ex-players on our regular *TMS* team, my era
was the late seventies and the eighties. I played for Leicestershire
against Tuffers' Middlesex for only two or three seasons before I
retired and we only got to know each other better when I started
covering England tours for the BBC.

Leicestershire lacked the resources of wealthier counties although,
when I made my debut in 1978, it had just enjoyed a golden era of
five trophies in five years – including the County Championship.
But, aside from a Benson & Hedges Cup win in 1985 and a County
Championship runners-up place in 1982, we saw precious few
silverware celebrations in the eighties despite regularly posting
respectable championship positions. During my 13 years at the club,
we finished eighth or better on ten occasions.

In terms of wealth, cricket in the 1970s was a planet apart from
today's game. For most players, it was a part-time summer
job – there was no IPL, central contracts, T20 or Hundred money
to plump up wage packets – and so from October to March you had
to hunt down any casual work going. Players would find themselves
doing shifts as lorry drivers, manual workers, shop assistants or
whatever else happened to be pasted in the local job centre window.
It was a perilous livelihood for most of the eighties and, until live
TV broadcasting money began to trickle down to the counties, you
were brave to see it as a viable career. But on Saturday 19 August
1978, I wasn't considering any of that as I prepared to make my first

team debut as 'Aggy' – my original nickname – this raw, fresh-faced 18-year-old kid. On that beautiful late-summer afternoon at Grace Road, who should my opponents be but none other than my Lancashire boyhood idols.

My mum and my brother were there but Dad couldn't come because he had a bad back. David Constant was umpiring, a man I'd only ever seen on the family telly, and in the dressing room I was rubbing shoulders with my captain Ray Illingworth and giants of the game like David Gower and Chris Balderstone. It all seemed like madness, completely unreal. I sat and watched as one of the West Indies' most lethal fast bowlers, Colin Croft, bowled at a thousand miles an hour, and there I was kitted out in schoolboy pads, green spiky gloves and no helmet; they weren't in widespread use. For a time, it looked like I was going to have to bat in the first innings, which would have been horrendous, but these were the days of 100-over compulsory declarations and thankfully we got through without me having to do it. There was still some time left at the end of the day so I was summoned to hurl down a few overs.

I was bowling down the hill at Grace Road with my long, Peter Lever-esque run-up and I was so excited that my very first delivery to England opener David Lloyd, aka Bumble, was a no-ball by at least a yard. Constant looked a bit nonplussed and said something like, 'Whoa back, young man,' and thankfully my next two were OK. Then came the fourth ball, which was to Bumble, and I have to say it was a magnificent delivery. It was a yorker, it swung, it was quick and it blew away his stumps. Off he went and everyone seemed a bit gobsmacked. Years later, I took a phone call at home from Bumble, now a close friend and then a Sky Sports commentator, which began with the words: 'Do you know what you were doing 25 years ago today, Agnew? I'll tell you. You got me out, you bastard.' And he put the phone down.

That August evening it rained in Leicester and because pitches were left uncovered in those days it meant we had a bowler-friendly surface on which to dismiss Lancashire cheaply the next morning. We made them follow-on, with the result that I spent two days of my first championship match in the field wearing plastic boots. I still didn't feel as though I belonged and one incident emphasised the gulf between professional cricket and the game I used to play. I was at mid-off when Ray Illingworth, who was in his final months as Leicestershire's captain, brought Jack Birkenshaw on to bowl up the hill at the legendary West Indian batsman Clive Lloyd. Jack set his field, Illy was at gully and just as the over was about to commence he suddenly bellowed: 'Hang on, Jack lad, look at this field. You're bowling uphill, it's a slow pitch and you're into the wind. Deep square has got to come round two yards.' A few balls later, Clive hit one straight down deep square's throat. I thought, my God, this is all a bit different.

One of the game's most respected and acidly observant cricket writers, the late Martin Johnson, reported that debut game for the *Leicester Mercury* and years later recalled his thoughts thus: 'It took him precisely four deliveries in county cricket to prove that he could knock over Test players, as well as sixth-formers, with his raw pace. David Lloyd's off stump flew so far back it almost impaled Roger Tolchard, the Leicestershire wicketkeeper. "Hello," we thought, "what have we got here?" Within months he had won a Whitbread Scholarship to Australia and more headlines followed there. Invited into an England net in Melbourne he promptly crusted the captain, Mike Brearley. It would have been better had he been able to serve his apprenticeship without so much national expectation, making steady rather than spectacular progress.'

Martin, who was a good friend, was spot on there. It all happened too fast and there was huge expectation, especially when Illingworth described me as the new Fred Trueman – a hell of a reputation to try and live up to. I was packed off to Australia with a vague assurance that someone called 'Frank' would meet me outside the airport arrivals hall. Again, none of our family had ever been near Australia and I emerged from my flight, blinking in the strong sunlight, feeling this was all a bit of a dream. That was emphasised when I discovered that 'Frank' turned out to be the former England bowler Frank 'Typhoon' Tyson, one of the quickest cricket has ever seen. By then, he'd emigrated to Australia and was coaching Victoria and I went to live with him for a month.

Frank was great for me. He sent me all over Victoria on weekdays with his coaches and had me back playing Grade Cricket at the weekends. Grade was tough. It was hard as nails, hot as hell, drinks only every hour – never on the outfield – and you had to grow up fast. I remember Keith Stackpole taking me on and enjoying it, and while we're good mates now we certainly weren't at the time. But I didn't grasp the enormity of any of this. I was still wallowing in the liberation of being away from Uppingham School – no uniform, no tie, no constantly being told what to do. I learned a lot on that trip, although there was no real training or mentoring in the way young players get today.

NICE LINE
Typhoon Tyson

Lancashire-born Frank 'Typhoon' Tyson is widely regarded as one of the fastest bowlers ever to hold a cricket ball. But speed isn't everything and, as Tyson's Test figures prove, he was also a thoughtful, aggressive and ruthlessly effective element of England's opening attack during the early 1950s. Among bowlers who have achieved 75 or more Test wickets, he has the seventh lowest average (76 wickets at 18.56) and no bowler since has claimed more than 20 wickets at a lower average.

An English Literature graduate of Durham University, Tyson was said to eschew sledging opponents in favour of quoting Wordsworth at them – he once allegedly deployed lines from Wordsworth's 'Simon Lee: The Old Huntsman' to inform a batter: 'For still, the more he works, the more/Do his weak ankles swell.' This must have been at once off-putting and mystifying. However, if any opponent saw Tyson as some kind of academic softie they were soon disabused. This certainly proved the case during only his second first-class game in 1953 against the touring Australians.

A young Aussie all-rounder, Richie Benaud, later revealed how his side had approached their game against Lancashire with the assurance that Tyson was a raw, untested young bowler who was not worth worrying about. That advice looked flaky from the moment Lancashire's wicketkeeper and slips stationed themselves halfway to the boundary and Tyson started his run from the opposite sightscreen. His first four balls could be summed up as: batter edges to boundary, batter is lbw before playing shot, new batter doesn't see ball whistle past nose, new batter's stumps are demolished and fly over wicketkeeper's head. So, no worries then.

The following year, Tyson earned his county cap and seemed only to have got quicker. One of his deliveries bounced once before hitting a sightscreen on the boundary behind on the full – a phenomenal feat recorded in the modern game only by the Australian paceman Jeff Thomson. That winter, Tyson toured Australia with MCC (England played overseas as the Marylebone Cricket Club) and although he made little impact in the 1st Test, he was outstanding in the 2nd. After being hit by a bouncer from another great fast bowler, Ray Lindwall, he had to be taken to hospital barely conscious. Tyson later recounted the episode in his book *In the Eye of the Typhoon*: 'He let me have a very fast, short-pitched delivery . . . Instinctively I turned a defensive back on the ball which skidded through and hit me a sickening blow on the back of my head. I sank to the ground and as I slipped in and out of consciousness, I was dimly aware of the players gathering round my prostrate body. Indistinctly I heard my fellow batsman Bill Edrich saying: "My God, Lindy, you've killed him!" . . . I was very, very angry with Ray Lindwall. And the whole of the Aussie team knew it . . . I would return the bouncer with interest.'

So he did but not, as the Australians suspected, via a barrage of lightning-fast, short-pitched bowling. Instead, Tyson took his revenge as a dish best served cold, returning to the game to pepper the home side with fast, full-pitched deliveries. With the hosts needing a reasonably comfortable 223 to win, he took them apart, claiming 6–85 to secure England a 38-run victory and ultimately a 3–1 series win.

I got home to find that Ray Illingworth was being replaced as
Leicestershire captain by my fellow digs resident Ken Higgs. It was a
well-deserved appointment for Ken who, at 42, went on to have a
glorious summer in his last full county season, finishing as fifth-
highest Englishman in the bowling averages. He was the chap who
had most influence on me in terms of technique – he was all about
basics, line and length, how to swing the ball, doing things
right – but he was also a giant of a man who clearly loved us.
However, the two characters at Grace Road who really turned me
into a potential international fast bowler were the West Indies'
Test player Andy Roberts, seriously quick by any standards, and
the England spinner Peter Willey. Peter, particularly, was hard as
nails. He used to beat Ian Botham at arm-wrestling. I would tease
him verbally and wind him up, and in retaliation he would either hit
me or force me to be nightwatchman. He knew I was terrified of
fast-bowling, particularly when it was served up by the West Indies
fast bowlers, then in their pomp, and he just loved watching me face
all that. If he was deputising as captain when David Gower was
away on England duty, I always knew what was coming. Much as I
hated it, and cursed him at times, Peter was and remains a dear
friend.

Being a nightwatchman did sometimes work in my favour. On one
occasion, we were at Scarborough playing Yorkshire, who didn't
have any genuinely fast bowlers, and I managed to block out until
the close. The next morning I launched an assault on Phil
Carrick, a left-arm spinner, and I'd knocked off about 60 runs
when a wicket fell and Peter Willey came out to bat. He was

muttering under his breath at how ridiculous it was that I'd scored so many – he really couldn't take it – and then promptly had his stumps blown out of the ground by Arnie Sidebottom for not very many. By then, I was around 70 not out. As he stomped past me back to the pavilion, I mischievously sought some advice: 'Will, any thoughts on how I should play?' I got a look of pure vitriol and a snarled 'Just keep f***ing going.' I did manage to get to 90 and was on course for the fastest century of the season, but then I nicked one off Paul Jarvis and was caught behind by David Bairstow.

After that, I was always going to get more stints as nightwatchman and, unfortunately for me, but no doubt perfect for Willey's *Schadenfreude*, it happened in a match against Hampshire. Hampshire's attack was rather different to Yorkshire's in the sense that they could deploy Malcolm Marshall, then arguably the most formidable member of the West Indies fast-bowling battery. They finished their innings, during which I'd bowled my boots off for 30 overs, and as I staggered into our changing room I heard Willey's voice in my ear: 'Come on, get your pads on. Malcolm's bowling so there'll be a wicket in a minute.' I pleaded: 'Oh, come on, Peter,' but I knew it was hopeless. I took as long as I could fastening my pads in the desperate hope that someone else could be nightwatchman if required. It was a forlorn wish. I had that feeling you get in the dentist's waiting room and I didn't have to wait long. A wicket fell and out I shuffled for my appointment with Malcolm Marshall.

Now, Malcolm is a lovely man on and off the field. He had hit me a couple of times in the past and always said sorry. But it was little consolation as his missiles zipped past my nose and thwacked into

Bobby Parks's gloves. At one point, I apparently looked up at the Grace Road pavilion with an expression frozen between trance-induced and terrified. What on earth was I doing out here? Then I got my answer because there was Peter laughing away on the pavilion balcony. At that point, I started thinking fast and so, a few balls later, when Malcolm unleashed another lethal bouncer which zoomed under my armpit, I put my plan into action.

In truth, my bat hadn't got within six inches of that ball. But then one of the fielders appealed excitedly – a strangulated, half-hearted appeal, on the lines of: 'Howzat? Oh, no, er, sorry.' That was good enough for me. I thought, sod it, and I walked off straight past Malcolm who looked thoroughly mystified and said: 'Where you going, man?' I gave him a high five and a 'well bowled' and walked off sharpish. Who should then come out to replace me but Peter Willey. He was absolutely fuming – 'You f***ing coward, Agnew. I'll get you for that.' He got hit all over his body for ten minutes, which didn't improve his mood. Sam Cook was the umpire and the next morning he sought me out: 'Thanks for walking, Aggy,' he said. 'I thought you got a little feather on that but I wasn't sure.' I'd got away with it but I knew Peter wouldn't forget.

The very next game we travelled to Chesterfield for a match against Derbyshire featuring one of the greatest fast bowlers ever to take the field. This was, of course, the man who in future years would become a regular *TMS* guest – Michael Holding, then nicknamed 'Whispering Death'. Michael had just taken the second new ball at Queen's Park, always a quick wicket, and it seemed incongruous that his opponents should have to endure physical torment in such a beautiful setting, fringed by trees and shrubs, iconic twisted church spire towering above one end. For me, it was a glorious view spoiled entirely by the sight of Michael running in to bowl.

As I walked out to bat in front of a big crowd – this was a Leicestershire–Derbyshire derby remember – I heard a shout from the pavilion: 'Hey, Aggy, you've forgotten summat.' It was Peter. I refused to be distracted and plodded on, only to hear a soft thud at my feet. To my dismay, he'd hurled a streaming toilet roll into my path. There were thousands watching and I still believe it was the most humiliating entry by any batsman in the history of first-class cricket. Sure enough, Willey had got his own back.

Of all the Windies quick bowlers, Sylvester Clarke was the most feared. He arrived wide at the crease, angled the ball in, bowled at the speed of light and would happily hit you. He enjoyed having the upper hand whereas Michael Holding wasn't bothered about small fry like me and Malcolm Marshall always apologised. Generally, the thinking was that if you bounced a fast bowler the message you sent was: 'I'm not bothered about you.' So if you were on the receiving end of that you got a bit stoked up. I never wanted to start a bouncer war with anyone but, in one case, involving yet another great West Indies' fast bowler in the shape of Wayne Daniel, I was ordered to do exactly that.

In June 1985 Peter Willey was deputising as Leicestershire captain in a match against Middlesex, for whom Wayne was the most potent attacking option. In our Lord's dressing room, Peter had told us in no uncertain terms to get stuck into him and I was in the middle of an over as he came out to bat. I remember thinking, 'I hope everyone's forgotten this stupid plan,' but of course Willey hadn't and shouted over from gully: 'Remember, Aggy, we're going to give him one.' So Wayne knew what was coming. He couldn't really bat but I bowled a kind of half-hearted bouncer, which he promptly smashed for six over deep point, an incredible shot. Next ball, thankfully, he was caught and you could hear comments from our lot such as 'That showed him.' We then heard the sound of Wayne hurling his bat across the home dressing room. He was absolutely furious. He ran in like a man possessed for three days and gave me a horrible time. Tuffers still loves recounting this, though at the time it was no laughing matter.

NICE LINE

Tuffers on making Wayne Daniel cross

Bowling bouncers at Wayne was always a bad idea. I wasn't in the Middlesex first team for that game against Leicestershire but I was on the ground staff and saw it all from the pavilion. Wayne had borrowed my bat and when Aggers bounced him he took a kind of duck-flurry hook and hit him for six. I was quite pleased with that because it showed what my bat could do and was probably the closest I'd get to hitting a six off Aggers. After that, the Leicestershire players were still winding Wayne up and I could see the smile spreading across Mike Gatting's face while other Middlesex players were shaking their heads, mystified, saying: 'Oh dear, why are they doing this?' Generally, it is a good idea to keep opposition quick bowlers sleepy rather than cross.

When Wayne stormed back into the dressing room, chucking my bat down without breaking stride, it was clear he was very cross. We knew an interesting passage of play lay ahead and he did not disappoint. He bowled at the speed of light and demolished the Leicestershire middle order, taking five wickets in four brutal overs. Even in their second innings, he hadn't calmed down. One bouncer hit Russell Cobb so hard on the helmet that one of the screws flew back over the bowler's head. And then he broke James Whitaker's arm, forcing him to retire hurt on 30. In the first innings, I can remember Aggers being manfully pushed out of the Leicestershire dressing room to go and face Wayne – apparently he took his guard squeaking: 'It was nothing to do with me. Willey told me to do it.' Fortunately, he was out pretty quickly to Phil Edmonds.

There are a couple of postscripts to Wayne's performance. Following his five-for, a wonderful photo appeared in next morning's *Daily Telegraph* showing a cricket ball with stumps exploding everywhere and not a batter in the bloody picture. You could just about see half a foot in the bottom corner, which was Gordon Parsons trying to get out of the way. The caption was something like: 'Daniel Mops Up Leicestershire'. Although Whitaker was hurt, not something any of us wanted to see, he so impressed Mike Gatting with his technique and bravery against quick bowling – he was the only one who tried to get behind the line of Wayne's deliveries – that Gatt got him on to the following year's successful Ashes tour to Australia. But it wasn't easy to break into a side that had the likes of Broad, Gower, Gatting and Lamb in its top order, and James only ever got to play one Test for England.

At Middlesex I used to field at mid-on to both Wayne and Angus Fraser. If there was a new ball, and Angus was bowling and the ball came to me, I could see the pitch scuffs all beautifully concentrated around the seam, which was where Angus landed it every time. When Wayne had the new cherry it would come to me with a leopard-skin pattern because he never much bothered about hitting the seam. It was all 'stick it in your hand and bowl fast'. Which he very much did. What a weapon he was for Middlesex.

My first months at Leicestershire were not just a huge cricket transition but also an insight into how professional cricketers interacted with each other personally. I was in a squad which predominantly comprised good county-level cricketers and – rising ever elegantly above them – the international superstar that was David Gower. David lived life on a completely different plane to the rest of us. But you would never hear him ramming that down your throat. He was a terrific colleague and I felt sorry for him when, during a large chunk of the 1980s, he became both England and Leicestershire captain. He'd finish a Test at Leeds on a Tuesday and be leading us out at Cardiff against Glamorgan on the Wednesday morning. It was a really tough ask and David was never that sort of character.

The players mostly got on fine together but you were still trying to get into the side at someone else's expense. At Surrey, that reality felt unhealthy, but it wasn't the case at Grace Road. Maybe it was the countryside vibe – Leicestershire is a rural county – but senior pros seemed more accepting of young cricketers and pleased when they did well. If you got a chance in the first team you had to make sure you took it and you were pretty cross if you later lost your place. Gordon Parsons and I were particularly competitive. Not only was he a year older than me but he had the temerity to be courting the daughter of our chief executive, Mike Turner, known to everyone as 'The Boss'. It seemed to me Gordon, who was a handy medium-fast bowler and useful lower-order batsman, had carved himself a bit of a head start.

We nicknamed him Bullhead. He looked a bit like the boxer Joe Bugner and had plenty of aggression when he was bowling. He also had this knack of knowing not only his own figures but everybody else's before we'd even walked off the outfield at the end of a long day. How the hell he did that I'll never know. But he and I shared a house together and we were mates.

My favourite Gordon story occurred around the time the ICC (International Cricket Council) brought in its one bouncer per over rule to restrict intimidatory bowling. Gordon's usual tactic was to bowl about five an over because he considered himself Leicestershire's answer to Dennis Lillee. During a game against Somerset at Grace Road, he removed one of the openers only to see Viv Richards striding to the wicket with trademark swagger, chewing gum, thumping the top of his bat handle and seeking out the opposing bowlers to stare them in the eye. Gordon wasn't the slightest bit fazed by that sort of stuff and his first ball was always going to be a bouncer. Viv knew that too and David Gower had even installed a man on the square-leg boundary for a possible hook catch. We were all set. Gordon came in, tearing down the hill and delivered his bouncer whereupon there was a sound like both barrels of a shotgun going off, followed by a very long silence.

There's a street called Milligan Road adjoining the cricket ground, and at the time a textile equipment manufacturer called Speizman Industries was based there. They had a glass roof and the ball sailed out of the ground to crash straight through it, loudly. Dickie Bird, who was umpiring, signalled six – one of the biggest any of us had ever seen – and then, as he was required to do, turned to Viv and said: 'I've called him, Viv lad, that's his one bouncer for the over.' Quick as a flash, Viv shouted back: 'No, Dickie. Tell him to bowl as many as he wants.' There was great on-field hilarity and Gordon was never allowed to forget it.

I always made it my business to get on with umpires and had a habit of popping into their dressing room before the start of county matches to see who was in charge. They're part of the game, they're often ex-players and they enjoy the banter as much as the rest of us. All that standing around must give them time to work on some one-liners because I found them pretty sharp with their on-field repartee. On one occasion, I told umpire Jack Bond, who had a great Lancastrian wit and was a childhood hero of mine, that the sun had caught his nose. 'You look like the red light outside a brothel, Jack,' I informed him. Bond replied: 'Well, we could all get under yours and not get sunburnt.' My old Leicestershire team-mate-turned-umpire Barry Dudleston would also relish an opportunity to comment on misfortunes that came my way. I once ran out my batting partner Phil Whitticase in a match against Gloucestershire and as he walked gloomily off Barry turned to me. 'Look on the bright side, Aggers,' he said, 'you're on your way to a five-for. You've got one wicket already.'

Cricket can be perceived as a 'posh' sport – to some eyes 'hijacked' by independent schools – but the truth is very different. In the north and Midlands it remains strongly rooted in what used to be called the working class and my main roomie for county away matches, Les Taylor, personified that tradition. Les was a former Bagworth Colliery coal miner who came late to the professional game and didn't play his first match for Leicestershire until he was 23. He was tall and powerful, and quickly became a first-team regular, eventually winning an England call-up after serving a three-year ban for joining Graham Gooch's 1982 rebel tour to South Africa.

I loved Les even though he took my place in the England side after I had a poor game in a howling gale in the 1985 Ashes Test in Manchester. He came in for the last match at the Oval and took the final wicket of the series, getting Ray Bright, caught and bowled. He was a terrific bowler, strong as an ox, and although utterly hopeless with the bat he nonetheless always insisted he was a whisker away from a decent innings. Before the start of every season he and I would hop into his white Morris Marina and drive down to Duncan Fearnley's bat factory in Worcester to get some much-coveted free sponsored kit. There would be three or four pairs of trousers or shirts laid out and Les would always enquire as to whether a new bat might be on offer? Duncan, a bit of a character himself, would sigh wearily and say, 'You had one last year, Les,' the unsaid point being that Les's previous bat couldn't have had much use. But Duncan would always reach under the rack, blow the dust off another one and hand it over.

NICE LINE
Les Taylor

Leicestershire and England seamer Les Taylor started working life as a miner at Bagworth Colliery, on the northwest Leicestershire coalfield, where according to workmates his breakfast-of-choice was a pork pie, a packet of crisps and a pint of bitter. Scooped up by Leicestershire at the age of 23 he quickly established himself as an accurate and effective county seam bowler and in 1981 bagged 75 wickets. But his England career never ignited. Ignored by selectors for the 1981–2 tour of India, he instead joined Graham Gooch's controversial rebel tour to South Africa – a decision that earned him a three-year ban from international cricket. When he returned, he played only two Tests for his country before persistent injuries dogged hope of a regular place.

Taylor, a career tail-ender, had a batting style best described as 'flailing'. One of his captains at Leicestershire, David Gower, was reportedly so concerned for his safety against quick bowling that, on one occasion, he opted to declare an innings rather than allow Taylor to bat. At the time, Leicestershire needed only 20 runs to save the follow-on but it would have meant Taylor having to face one of the West Indies' quickest and most aggressive bowlers, Sylvester Clarke. In the dressing room, Gower turned to his senior players, shook his head and said: 'I just can't do it.'

In the eighties, the county circuit was like a raucous family constantly on the road. Away from home, players would be berthed in a Trusthouse Forte or Posthouse hotel – the equivalent of today's Premier Inn and Travelodge – and have dinner at a Berni Inn, a then ubiquitous restaurant chain. Astonishingly, a Berni steak would often be the fourth square meal of the day. The counties took great pride in their reputation for hospitality and at most venues players would be treated to a sumptuous roast dinner for lunch followed by sandwiches and cakes for tea. The Middlesex and England captain Mike Gatting was known to be the foremost trencherman on the circuit and his particular fondness for Branston's pickle – he had it with virtually everything – was the source of much amusement. A few weeks after he received his OBE from the Queen, I felt compelled to stick my head around the visitors dressing room to congratulate him on being recognised as an Obese Branston Eater.

Obviously, diet had to change in the professional game and in the mid-1980s Kent's coach Brian Luckhurst became the first in England to introduce the notion of healthy and nutritious menus. Lunch at Kent would perhaps mean pasta with a bit of salad and as a fast bowler in need of sustenance you'd feel uncertain about that because you're obviously using a lot of calories. But Brian was right and, although he was widely ridiculed, he was way ahead of his time. Bizarrely, although you'd think diet would be the first and most obvious way to improve performances, Leicestershire opted for a more 'alternative' approach. In 1987 we were sent off to be hypnotised.

Whereas most counties would embark on a pleasant pre-season tour to the Caribbean or somewhere, we drove off to the Isle of Wight and the Farringford Hotel. This was apparently the historic home of Alfred Lord Tennyson and the preferred holiday bolthole for our boss, Mike Turner. It was all a bit bizarre but the bottom line was that we had been underperforming. We were a good side. We'd won the Benson & Hedges in 1985 but we hadn't even threatened the championship. We were better than that and it was felt hypnotism might offer something a bit different to help kickstart a turnaround in fortunes. So, although slightly sceptical, we duly lay on the floor while the hypnotist Martin Landau-North put us under.

We were given the key word 'shovel'. The idea was that whenever we felt under pressure in a game, David Gower would shout that word out and we would mentally shovel the pressure back on to the opposition. Gower was the most unlikely person to be involved in this sort of stuff but he went along with it. I'm not sure it worked terribly well; it wasn't much good if you were being smashed all over the field. But it was an interesting experiment and innovative for the mid-eighties. Besides, I smoked in those days and whatever Mr Landau-North said to me while I was in a hypnotic state certainly curbed that – at least for a while.

During matches, long hours spent waiting to bat or for rain to cease would be enlivened with card games such as Sweaty Betty. We'd play it all the time – me, Gordon Parsons, Peter Willey and Andy Roberts. The idea was to get as few points as possible and Willey used to keep the scores in his cricket boot all season; tens of thousands of points were carefully recorded. Every card counted for its face value but the Queen of Spades, i.e. Sweaty Betty, was worth 50. You could pass three cards around, including the Queen, so you were basically stitching up the player next to you. You had to do it with a straight face but Andy Roberts could never manage that and would produce this great, guttural chuckle whenever he managed to pass on Sweaty Betty.

On the field, there were certain teams you always felt confident against and vice versa. I don't think I ever took many wickets at Lord's but I always got them at the Oval and always when playing against Kent. The counties were up against each other quite regularly so, if you got a decent haul of wickets, opponents would treat you with more trepidation in future. I loved playing on the Kent festival grounds such as Canterbury, Tunbridge Wells and Folkestone, I enjoyed Gloucester and Cheltenham and I still have a strong affection for Yorkshire's county grounds – I think I've played at every one of them. I also enjoyed discovering new places to play, such as the Welsh grounds at Ebbw Vale, Llandudno and Llanelli. After games, stalwart fans would come up for a chat or an autograph, their faces often recognisable from previous encounters, and this interaction was considered by county administrators part and parcel of a player's duties.

Some supporters were so cricket-obsessed that I suspected they would turn up even when no game was listed. Dot, for instance – I never knew her second name – would sit on her deckchair by the players' gate at Grace Road, opening and shutting it as batsmen came and went. She never missed a match. Then there was a chap called Chris who would bawl support as he shuffled around the stands, unfortunately always with wet trousers. I loved going down to the boundary and exchanging opinions with our supporters because, to many of them, Leicestershire was as much their home as their club. They felt they were among friends. There would always be a lot of banter flying around, especially noticeable when I was sitting on the advertising hoardings at fine leg.

At Derby, there was an infamous Grumblers' Corner which produced hilarious comments to help enliven a long day in the field. To my mind, this was a cherished part of the whole county tradition. But then everything became more serious and it was decreed by the powers-that-be that I shouldn't be engaging with supporters during games and needed to be fully focused on my performance. In fact, I was always fully focused. I was just trying to kill a bit of time during breaks in play. There definitely came a point when, under Graham Gooch's captaincy, England adopted a more professional set-up and that probably influenced the counties. I found I had to put that 'boundary banter' side of me away.

You don't see the same engagement with fans now and neither do you between the players. We would always, at least once every match, meet the opposition in the pub, and I would sit and listen in awe to bowlers like Richard Hadlee and Malcolm Marshall chatting away. They weren't people who wanted to down pint after pint and, as I didn't even drink in those days, I would be there nursing a Coke. Meeting your oppos socially involved a kind of unwritten agreement. You'd have an evening as friends and colleagues in the pub but the next day you'd be back at the cricket hammer and tongs.

I've had this conversation with Stuart Broad many times because he's always been convinced that we went out to get completely zonked. But that just wasn't true. Most of the time, we were talking cricket and if any stuff had happened on the field – a bit of a row perhaps – it would usually get put away. Occasionally, animosity would rumble on, such as when Ian Greig accused me of being a 'chucker' – shorthand for using a prohibited bowling action – which is the biggest insult you can fire at a bowler. No-one had ever said that about me before and I actually thought I had quite a good action. When Ian wrote that, it hurt. There were some quite hostile games between us for a while but we eventually sorted it out over a drink.

In my experience, sledging rarely upset anyone and was mostly a fun way for the fielding side to pass the time. It was never about being vicious or abusive – far better to try and disrupt a player's focus. Whenever I was batting against Northamptonshire, Allan Lamb, from his slip position, always used to be in my ear chuntering on about turkey rustlers and whether my dad's turkey farm had enough protection. I was once even 'sledged' while bowling courtesy of Graeme 'Foxy' Fowler who, as non-striker, told me as I walked back to my mark: 'Hey, Aggy, did you know your cheeks wobble when you run in?' And I found myself sucking in my cheeks for the next ball. He stood there, leaning on his bat, with that ridiculous smile of his, saying: 'You're still doing it. They're still wobbling.' He finished me. It's not about being rude or nasty. It's about getting inside a player's head and putting him off.

Dear old Monte Lynch, another good mate, would come out batting for Surrey, wide-eyed under his helmet, and know I was going to bowl him a series of wide half-volleys outside off stump. He would leave ball after ball alone and I'd be saying, 'Come on, Monte, you know you want to.' Eventually he'd succumb, have a great whoosh with his bat and he'd be gone. I love hostility and aggression on the field, and as a fast bowler you've got to turn yourself into that animal. But sledging? I don't even like the word. Yes, you occasionally heard racist and similarly unacceptable stuff from certain people but generally it was rare.

Far more common, given the amount of time players of the same team spent in each other's company, were the internal spats. One which hit the headlines at the start of the 1988 season involved myself and my Leicestershire and England team-mate Phil 'Daffy' DeFreitas. It was a brief toys-out-of-the-pram moment which got horribly overplayed by the media. Yet it did illustrate the kind of petty dressing-room bust-up which is usually so carefully shielded from the press.

I'd been ill in bed for a few days and returned to a game at Grace Road against Sussex in case I was needed to bat to try and save the match. Our chef had prepared a light fish lunch especially for me and, as I prepared to tuck in, Daffy walked over, picked up a salt cellar and shook it over the plate. It wasn't his fault, but the top was loose and the whole lot came out, ruining the only food I could face. To get my own back, I nipped upstairs and emptied his kit bag over the balcony. Unfortunately, my old cricket teacher at school, Garth Wheatley, a former Surrey player, was pottering about below and

Daffy's bat nearly killed him with a direct hit. Daffy left the ground in a huff, forcing Mike Turner to go and find him and drag him back. He then batted brilliantly to smash the winning runs. Daffy and I were constantly in competition but we have always been mates and I felt sorry for him afterwards. Unbelievably, the whole episode was splashed across the front of the *Daily Mirror* – 'England Stars in Bust-Up' or something.

Daffy was an extraordinarily talented cricketer but wasn't always the easiest player to manage – especially when Peter Willey was involved. Peter had no real concept of diplomacy and, during one 1987 team meeting called by David Gower to tackle Leicestershire's generally lacklustre performance, he accused DeFreitas of 'not trying' during a Sunday League game against Sussex. Daffy hit back, insisting he had been ill, but a meeting designed to rejuvenate players rapidly degenerated to achieve the opposite.

At that time, Daffy was in the England side and Peter liked to ensure that he and the other England players – namely Chris Lewis and myself – had our feet kept firmly on the ground. Peter could be very encouraging but he was also fond of geeing people up through criticism. That kind of goading approach doesn't always work and Andy Roberts certainly resented being wound up in a similar manner by one or two of his Hampshire team-mates, who would offer comments such as: 'Come on, you're supposed to be a fast bowler.' It was counterproductive and Andy didn't forget it. After he left Hampshire for us, those same players got none-too-subtle reminders of quite how quick he was.

To accuse a fast bowler of not trying because he's not bowling his fastest is ridiculous. It's very simplistic to equate effort with speed and that's why it is absurd to expect, say, Jofra Archer to bowl at 90 mph all the time. He can bowl that fast but he's very rhythmical and just because he's not hitting 92 mph it doesn't mean he's not trying. I know myself that you can be working your hardest to bowl as quick as you can only to discover it isn't happening. The ball doesn't come out right, the rhythm isn't there.

In situations like that you need a sensible, thoughtful captain. From a bowling perspective, David Gower was my dream captain because he would let you set your own field, do your own thing and intervene only when he thought it necessary. There was no fiddling about with field changes before you'd even walked back to your mark. He encouraged people to think for themselves and that made them better cricketers. Having said that, we didn't always see eye-to-eye and one of our biggest rows came in May 1988 as I was loosening up to open the bowling against Kent. Gower told me that, instead, DeFreitas would open with our other quick seamer, George Ferris. I was furious. It was the first time as a pro I'd been denied use of the new ball and I considered it the nearest thing to being dropped. I sulked at fine leg for two sessions, although as it turned out it was probably a neat bit of psychology because David tossed me the ball straight after tea and I ripped through their top order to return 6–37.

In hindsight, I was wrong to react as I did. I needed the new ball to bowl well, I'd taken loads of wickets with it the previous season and I was obsessed with fighting my way back into the England team. It wouldn't happen now but, at the time, with a few decent performances, you could suddenly find yourself getting picked. Nonetheless, David was quite entitled to give someone else a go or indeed give me a prod. I was selfish. I was thinking too much of myself, and the more cricket you watch the more you realise it's a team game.

Gower had two other great assets as far as the rest of us were concerned. Firstly, he was self-evidently one of the best batsmen in the world and so was perpetually the centre of attention. And secondly, his blond curls made him instantly recognisable. He just attracted everybody. So we developed this subtle skill, deployed whenever we came off the field or left a nets session, to make sure he always went first. He would be surrounded by hundreds of people, allowing us to quietly make our way around the fringes untroubled by any demands from the public.

He was never a voracious netter and never needed to be, given his ability. Occasionally, he'd have a net if he was unhappy about something – moving his feet perhaps – but frankly, net surfaces were not great in the eighties and you could do yourself more harm than good if a quick ball reared up. I netted to warm up but that was it. My old *TMS* colleague Fred Trueman always relished pointing out that he bowled far more overs than me during his career and, while that's true, my generation bowled many more than players do today. We bowled ourselves fit and we didn't break down as much. It is true that players are now better athletes and I'm envious of the time put into developing their game. They get a lot of coaching, video analysis, the lot, and I'd have loved all that. I recently asked Mark

Wood if he felt some of us on *TMS* talked nonsense because we'd never experienced the way players are coached today. He assured me it wasn't the case.

By the end of the eighties, I was becoming ever-more frustrated at the lack of an England recall. I'd had my best-ever season in 1987, with over 100 first-class wickets, and then another consistent run in 1988 when I was third-highest county wicket taker. Yet the selectors apparently didn't notice. I briefly got my hopes up towards the end of the 1989 home Ashes series when, with England 4–0 down, Gower decided as a late afterthought that I should be playing in the final Test because England's established fast bowlers had all been pulling out with injuries. He even told me to go home to get my kit ready. But then, the following morning, he called saying that his fellow selectors, Micky Stewart and Ted Dexter, had overruled him.

That was a shattering blow and I knew my international career was over. I'd already spent a winter working as sports producer for BBC Radio Leicester and on 7 September 1988 even made a debut appearance on *TMS* as guest summariser during a Refuge Assurance semi-final between Worcestershire and Middlesex. That was a quite terrifying experience, although I at least had the advantage of being a new summariser with fresh stories about the players and some unheard anecdotes. It gets harder when you've been doing it for years, which is why I so admire Vic Marks. He may not know today's players well but he has a good, current knowledge of everything that's going on.

Finally, in the spring of 1990, with Leicestershire stalling over my request for an increased salary of £15,000, I made up my mind. I accepted an offer from the *Today* newspaper to take up a permanent staff position as cricket correspondent and played my last County Championship game for Leicestershire against Derbyshire at the end of that season. Weeks later, I was heading off with the England team, which included a 24-year-old debutant called Phil Tufnell, to cover the 1990–1 Ashes tour in Australia. That tour gave me some fantastic experience – not least because I worked alongside experienced tabloid journalists and cricket writers – although it resulted in me again jumping ship, this time to become the BBC's cricket correspondent. That career move was, bizarrely, triggered by a very public row between Tuffers and the tour management, more of which in Chapter 6. And, equally bizarrely, my shiny new media career would be briefly interrupted by one last hurrah as a first-class cricketer, as we shall see in the next chapter.

TOP LIST
Worst 15 Feb 2022

AGGERS Matthew Hoggard. Usually did his job but hung around tediously too long next morning!

TUFFERS That would be me. I only did it once, for Middlesex away at Sussex. I was racked off at being given the nightwatch job so I had a huge swipe at my first ball from Tony Pigott and got a four over the slips. Unfortunately, the next one smashed the middle pole out of the ground, which forced my skipper Mike Gatting out to bat. He was not happy.

ISA I honestly don't know. I can tell you the best, though – Jason Gillespie, who ended up scoring a double century in Bangladesh. I know because he often reminds me.

EBONY Don't know about the worst but the funniest must have been Tuffers. I've never seen anyone hop around so much at the crease.

CARLOS The West Indies' Alzarri Joseph. He would want to be playing all the shots instead of batting things out.

AATIF There are too many bad ones to recall but England's best was Alex Tudor – 99 not out in his third Test match and hardly ever picked again.

CHAPTER 4

COUNTY SET – NINETIES AND NOUGHTIES

In which Phil breaks the breakfast rules
and Aggers makes an unlikely comeback.

TUFFERS

During the early nineties, Middlesex made the running in the County Championship, taking the title in 1990 and 1993 and the Sunday League in 1992. My experienced England team-mate John Emburey and myself were dubbed the 'spin twins' – a title which, for my part, was inherited from John's former spin partner Phil Edmonds – and we came into our own during hot summers when dry wickets most suited the spinning ball. With our long-serving captain and England batter Mike Gatting at the helm, world-class players like Mark Ramprakash and Desmond Haynes at the top of the order, and England seamer Angus Fraser leading the seam attack, Middlesex were English cricket's big beast. And this was all on the back of an impressive 1980s, which saw us take three County Championship titles, three Gillette/NatWest trophies and two Benson & Hedges Cups.

As a teenager I was on Middlesex's radar but it wasn't until 1985 that the club began to show real interest in signing me. Emburey's former spin partner Phil Edmonds was nearing the end of his career, a replacement was required and as I was already on the Marylebone Cricket Club ground staff at Lord's I had a bit of a leg up. I'd been working under MCC head coach Don Wilson, who I think tipped off the Middlesex head coach Don Bennett, suggesting I was worth a look. I was told I would be 'watched' in an upcoming MCC match against Surrey, that it was my big chance and I shouldn't waste it. Not that I took much notice. If you were to look for a job interview analogy, it would be a candidate who looked sulky, refused to engage, shouted and swore a lot and then snatched his CV off the interviewer to rip into minuscule pieces.

Don Wilson was captaining MCC that day and for some reason I manoeuvred myself into a blazing on-field argument with him. I was obviously nervous and when I began with a few bad deliveries, I blamed the runs I conceded on Don's field placings. It was ridiculous but it was a row that fast got out of proportion and Don was never going to concede to a mouthy kid. So he removed me from the attack, ordered me to field at fine leg both ends – a humiliatingly long trek between overs – and then brought himself on to show how it should be done. I reckon he'd only intended to have a couple of overs to teach me a lesson but then thought to himself, well, the ball's coming out rather nicely, I'll keep going. And he did. All afternoon. Don Bennett was no doubt bewildered at being summoned out to Hampstead to watch a 50-year-old Yorkshireman bowl. For my part, I thought Don Wilson was mugging me off, making me look stupid in front of my prospective new boss and ruining my chance of a Middlesex contract.

It got worse. As I worked myself into a state of self-justifying indignation at fine leg, I suddenly saw an opportunity to get my own back. As the ball rolled my way, I trapped it, football style, and booted it back to the wicketkeeper, accompanied by a broadside of assorted swearwords. Hands-on-hips, an understandably furious Wilson fired back a laser stare while Bennett simply headed for his car. And yet, hard though it is to believe, even this unsavoury spectacle failed to destroy my chances. Determined to at least see me bowl, Bennett had me picked to play for Middlesex 2nds in a two-innings match against Hampshire at Southampton.

This was staged on a 'green' wicket suited to seam rather than spin and our quick bowlers tore through the opposition, giving me little chance to show what I could do. Eventually Bennett buttonholed our captain Keith Tomlins during a break in play and basically ordered him to put me on. In such moments, I suppose, sporting careers stand or fall. I was summoned into the attack, returned figures of 6 for 36 and days later I signed for Middlesex. Don Bennett could so easily have walked away thinking I was more trouble than I was worth but he persevered, and I suspect this was because Don Wilson gave him the nod and explained that at Hampstead he'd been trying to knock some rough edges off me. I had talent, which people could see, but talent without application isn't ever enough. I was lucky in that, throughout my career, people always seemed to give me one more chance.

Over the next three years, I increasingly featured alongside John Emburey in the Middlesex attack. I played only two championship matches in 1986 but the following year claimed 31 wickets in eight games at an average of 30.29 and then, in 1988, 22 in nine games at 36.14. But it was in 1989 (50 in 13 at 29.1) and 1990 (65 in 20 at 34.72) that I suppose I emerged as a leading spin bowler. That hot summer of 1990, with its turning pitches, helped pave the way for an England call-up although, if the selectors knew what they were buying into, it might have been a mighty different story. In those apprenticeship years with Middlesex I was still playing the teenage rebel, winding up my captain and other senior players whenever the mood struck. Sometimes I would adopt a diametrically opposite approach to the one which got me into hot water with Don Wilson back in 1985. Here I was in a team with Mike Gatting and John Emburey. I can hear myself as a young kid saying to them: 'You're the bloody England captain and vice-captain. You're the ones who know what's going on. You set the bloody field.' But that wasn't clever because, of course, you've got to work things out in your own head.

I had quite a good eye for spotting a batter's weakness and mostly captains left it to me to decide how best to attack. Later in my career, I was much more open to listening to ideas and my go-to guys were my keepers and my first slips. They could see exactly how a batter was playing you and would give you feedback. Gatt was never one for concocting a detailed tactical bowling plan. The plan tended to be unerringly simple: 'Just get him out.' We'd sit in endless team meetings talking about a particular batter being vulnerable to short-pitched bowling or why we needed an extra gully but the conclusion was always the same. Aim for the top of off stump and hold your catches. That said, bowling is no different to any other job in the sense that you develop during your career and you learn to try different things as the situation requires. I didn't have any special plan for bowling at Michael Vaughan, though, because I was a bit older than him and he was still finding his way in county cricket. I do recall getting him out at Lord's with a beauty though – pitched leg stump, took the top of off. It's possible I remind him of that occasionally.

In the Middlesex changing room, my nickname was Scruffnell because I had this long hair, a ponytail, an earring and the general aura of being a bit of a raver. I would also get frequent bollockings for having a quiet catnap in the dressing room if we were batting – a habit that earned me my nickname 'The Cat'. But I was also starting to get some attention for my performances on the field and one day Gatt came over saying that the England manager Micky Stewart was coming to watch me at Uxbridge. He suggested I spruce up, play the part, wear a clean pair of trousers – all the usual stuff – and that although he didn't personally care how long my hair was, I had to bloody well sharpen my look if I wanted to play for England. I think I grunted back something like: 'What do you know' and 'If they want me, they'll pick me.' So when I turned up looking a bit rough, Gatt frogmarched me kicking and screaming to his car, drove to the nearest barber shop, removed my earring and ordered a short-back-and-sides.

I bowled well at Uxbridge, got a five-for I think, and a month later I was picked for England. I've got a lot to thank Gatt for. He taught me it's not all about running up and taking wickets or smashing runs. You've got to conduct yourself as a professional cricketer. In county cricket, I couldn't have asked for a better, more straightforward skipper. He could give you a bollocking on Monday after your dire weekend performance and the fact that you looked the worse for wear, but by Tuesday morning it would all be forgotten. He never bore a grudge and professionally he managed players as well as anyone. Much harder would have been trying to manage my personal life.

In those first years at Middlesex, mine was, to put it mildly, challenging. My marriage was falling apart – something I've written about in some detail over the years – and there were plenty of evenings when I never made it home. Fortunately, the Lord's cook was none other than Nancy Doyle, a matriarchal Irishwoman whose lunches and teas were considered the finest on the county circuit.

My record for devouring her lamb chops was 15 in a single lunch break and I have no idea how I managed to leave my chair, let alone play cricket, after that. Nancy also conjured up the best steak-and-kidney pudding you ever tasted, served with mashed potato and peas, followed by spotted dick and custard. If we were bowling, we didn't always have the spotted dick but we'd still walk out from the pavilion wanting a kip. Our fielding performances tended to dip a touch during afternoon sessions.

Nancy probably saved my life at that time because I was going through a divorce, my mum had not long died of leukaemia and I wasn't looking after myself very well. She would find me asleep in the car before a game – I wouldn't have necessarily gone home – hoik me out and drag me inside for breakfast. She saw me as a skinny, bedraggled, somewhat bewildered youth who needed to be taken under her wing. And thank God she did.

During county games, only the senior Middlesex players, the likes of Gatt and Emburey, were allowed breakfast at Lord's and they would get served a full English fry-up. Nancy would sit me down in the dining room with them and ensure I got the same. However, on one occasion it so happened that one of the posher Middlesex committee men was in there talking to Gatt as I tucked in. This chap rather pompously informed Nancy that 2nd XI players – i.e. Philip Tufnell – weren't normally allowed in the dining room, to which Nancy, a straight-talking Irishwoman who did not bother taking prisoners, replied: 'Fock off, both of youse. Can you not see the boy needs food?' Duly castigated, they had to watch disapprovingly as I demolished another delicious rasher of bacon.

NICE LINE
Nancy Doyle, matriarch of the cricket tea

A glorious and oft-overlooked fact is that cricket is the only sport with lunch and tea enshrined in its rules. Law 11.2.1 states: 'An interval for lunch or tea shall be of the duration determined under Law 2.3 (Consultation with captains), taken from the call of Time before the interval until the call of Play on resumption after the interval.' It's unclear why this isn't Law 1.0.0 considering that clubs at all levels take huge pride in their culinary offerings. Whatever, of all the great cooks to grace a pavilion kitchen, the late Annie Gertrude Doyle MBE, known universally as Nancy, was perhaps the greatest.

Raised in Mullingar, in Ireland's Midlands, she was head cook at Lord's from the mid-sixties until her retirement in 1996. Diminutive in size, but a pocket-rocket in terms of feistiness, her reputation for traditional home-cooked meals (no mung beans or quinoa here) was legendary while the size of her portions contributed to a certain lethargy among fielding teams. This was not lost on Oxbridge-educated Middlesex and England captain Mike Brearley, who repeatedly tried to persuade Nancy that soup, starter, roast lamb, roast potatoes, chips, veg, dessert (with a choice of custard or ice cream) and a cheeseboard was not the ideal diet for professional athletes. Brearley's team-mate and former *Guardian* cricket correspondent Mike Selvey later summed up the conversation in a tweet:

Brearley: 'You're giving my players too much'. Nancy (5ft and v Irish): 'Tell you what. You don't tell me how to feed my boys and I won't tell you how to fockin' bat. OK?'

Although I was having a rough ride outside cricket, the dressing room proved a sanctuary. I had Gatting to play a father-figure role and Emburey to give me the kind of advice that, over the next 12 years, would help me claim over 1000 first-class wickets. John would say things that, although they seem obvious looking back, never even occurred to me. For instance, on my debut at Worcestershire in June 1986, I couldn't understand how Graeme Hick, Dipak Patel and Phil Neale were able to consistently smash me through the covers when I was landing balls on a good length, just outside off stump, with a bit of decent spin. These were deliveries straight out of the coaching manual, the essence of leg-spin theory, so why was I being despatched for an embarrassingly expensive six-an-over for figures of 13–3–76–0? John hadn't played in the game – both he and Gatting were on duty for England in the 1st Test against India – but the following week he called me over for what he called 'a word of advice, take it or leave it'.

Embers reminded me that Hick was in his pomp, Neale was a gnarled old county pro, Worcestershire were top of the league and I'd bowled on as flat a track as any batter could wish for. Hick and Neale had been able to use their feet to come down the wicket and I'd made their job easier because I'd been too predictable. I needed to watch the way people played. Someone might have a lovely cover drive but that might also be the only decent shot they had. In which case, I should bowl straighter, change my pace, produce an arm ball, drop a bit shorter. Above all, I should not keep doing the same thing, however 'textbook' it was. I just thought: 'Bloody hell. There's a more to this then.' At 20, it was a transformational moment. And the truth is, as a spinner, it takes you ten years to get the hang of it.

Of course, there were still days when nothing worked and I would have to turn to my regular dressing-room mucker and future England team-mate Angus Fraser for some mutual consolation. I used to sit next to Gus in both the Middlesex and England dressing rooms and he always swore blind that he was the unluckiest player ever to step on to a cricket field. No-one ever held catches off him, the fielders were useless, the umpires undermined him by refusing to give clear lbw decisions. I loved Big Angus, a man who looked as exhausted after his first over as he did when he trudged off at the end. In fairness, I was close behind him in the moaning stakes. At times we would be grumbling on to each other like those two cantankerous characters in *The Muppets*, Statler and Waldorf.

Looking back I reckon that if the Decision Review System (DRS) had been going in the nineties – with all the ball-tracking technology now available through Hawkeye – we would both have got a couple of hundred more lbw decisions. As it was, I had to rely on a bit of barrack-room psychology provided by my old coach Don Wilson. It was a kind of three-card trick aimed at getting the umpire on your side. The first time your appeal is turned down you're all: 'Sorry about that, ump. Just thought it might have clipped leg stump. I can see you got that right though.' Second time it's: 'Cor blimey, ump, that one must have been tight but, fair enough.' And then the third time you say: 'Surely that one's got to be plumb, ump?' And surprisingly often it would work. I've ended up on my knees many times in front of umpires, pleading for the finger to rise, although some bowlers try appealing without even a glance back at them – as though the batter is so obviously out that it's a fait accompli – and run off to celebrate. Stuart Broad deployed that tactic in his youth until he realised it was giving umpires the hump. I found out too late that buying your umpire an after-match drink in the bar was also a vital part of the buttering-up process.

Throughout the nineties, I became an automatic pick for Middlesex and, aside from one lay-off in 1992, I stayed remarkably injury free. The only serious problem I suffered happened in a Nottinghamshire v. Middlesex game at Trent Bridge in 1992. I came off at lunchtime feeling particularly rough and a few minutes later somebody found me on the floor in the toilets in excruciating pain and convulsing. I was carted off in an ambulance and it turned out to be a burst appendix. Thankfully my rescuer was not a Middlesex player – had he been, I'd probably have been accused of trying to avoid bowling on a flat track. Generally, apart from a few niggles, I was very lucky with injuries. But, like I've always said, if you haven't got muscles you can't pull 'em.

My prowess as a left-arm spinner was rarely called into question by team-mates but my batting, particularly against fast bowling, was the source of some comic relief. In that debut game at Worcester in 1986 I felt a distinct stab of panic as I plodded slowly out at No. 11 to face my first County Championship ball from Neal Radford, who would not mind me saying that he was hardly in the fearsome category. I was informed later that, as Neal ran in to bowl, the fielders could see the helmet shaking on top of my head. Even so, I scratched 8 runs – not the worst debut for a tail-ender – before getting run out in a last-man stand with Angus.

I used to love batters because they were my wall of defence before the bloody fast bowlers could have a go at me. I made sure they had everything they could ever want: took them out for a pint, bought them a bit of dinner and reminded them how important it was for them to look after their tail-end spinner. Mike Gatting did try me as nightwatch, just the once, for an away match against Sussex. I was a bit racked off at being given the job so I had a huge swipe at my first ball from Tony Pigott and got a four over the slips. Unfortunately, his next one smashed my middle pole out of the ground and that spelled trouble because it meant Gatt was forced to come out and bat for the dying minutes of play. He muttered something darkly Anglo-Saxon to me as we crossed on the outfield and I could see a proper rollocking brewing. I was showered, changed and heading for the team hotel before he even got back to the pavilion.

THE 1992 AGGERS COMEBACK

AGGERS

By 1992, I'd been out of first-class cricket for two years and my sole day job was being BBC cricket correspondent. I'd been covering an England v. Pakistan ODI at Trent Bridge and was just about to interview Graham Gooch when he suddenly said: 'Are you really going to play in the semi-final then, Aggy? I'll smack you everywhere.' That was the first I'd heard about a one-off comeback game for Leicestershire in their NatWest Trophy semi-final against Gooch's Essex. Next thing I knew, the Leicestershire captain Nigel Briers was on the phone brushing off my complaints that I hadn't bowled for two years and saying: 'Even if you end up getting 0-100 and drop three catches it will be the right decision.' So I had no choice after that.

Our coach Jack Birkenshaw said some nice things about me being a high-class bowler and wishing I could play full-time, but I didn't want to look a fool. I was only medium-pace by this time and although I'd played a couple of charity matches those were a world away from a NatWest Trophy semi-final. I went to the nets the day before the game, had a short bowl – I knew I'd be stiff if I bowled too many – and took a few catches. But that was it in terms of practice. I just turned up for the match hoping I could get through 12 overs. What I didn't know is that my mates in the press box had charitably organised a sweepstake on how many runs I'd go for. Someone backed 100-plus, which seemed a little unkind but I suppose it gave them a laugh.

We bowled first and three things went my way. First, our West Indian quick bowler Winston Benjamin got Gooch out cheaply for 8, which put his threat to smash me around the ground out of the equation. Then, when my very first ball was drilled to point, with four runs written all over it, Winston made a brilliant stop, denying Essex even a single. That made all the difference because, if that ball had gone to the boundary, it would have sent a signal that my bowling could be pilloried. And thirdly, Nasser Hussain was terrified to get out to me and blocked every delivery. I later found out that David Gower and Ray Illingworth, who were both commentating for telly, kept mischievously changing the screen caption when I was on. It went from 'Jonathan Agnew, right arm fast' in my first over to 'Jonathan Agnew, right arm slow' in my last.

When I finally finished my spell and wandered wearily down to fine leg, my old pal David Lloyd, who was working for the *Evening Standard*, suddenly popped out from behind a rose bush and said: 'You won't believe this. I've got to get a quote from you.' I had at least produced acceptable figures of 12–2–31–1, I didn't concede a boundary and in a rain-affected final Leicestershire won by five wickets with a ball to spare. It was all worth it to see a Mahood cartoon in the *Daily Mail* the next day which had Graham Gooch, hands in his pockets, sloping off the field with a team-mate above the caption: 'It's bad enough these commentators telling us how to play without coming out and showing us.'

NICE LINE

The press on Aggers' comeback

My effort was encapsulated by my old friend Martin Johnson, who wrote in *The Times*: 'Agnew continued to bowl tightly, although as each over passed the walk back to third man became progressively more weary and the swigs from his drinking bottle ever more frequent. As his normal tipple now is gin and tonic, interspersed with the occasional small cigar, this was hardly surprising.'

In a curious postscript I was in the BBC commentary box for the Leicestershire v. Northamptonshire final alongside Peter Willey, who I'd corralled into acting as summariser. As we were chatting, we spotted Nigel Briers frantically waving at us from below, the signal that a new crisis had emerged. Leicestershire bowler Vince Wells had been taken to hospital after collapsing with chest pains and David Millns had injured his back during early net practice. Briers now wanted myself and Willey to step into the breach. Leaving aside the obvious point – that the BBC would be somewhat lightly staffed for a major sporting event – I was having none of it. I'd got away with the semi-final, perhaps on reputation, and I certainly wasn't going to risk it again. Registration forms were rushed through for Willey but he was stood down when David recovered sufficiently to bowl. Vince made a full recovery after hospital tests and the only real casualty on the day was Leicestershire – thrashed by eight wickets.

TOP LIST
Deadliest spinner

AGGERS Can't choose between Shane Warne and Muttiah Muralitharan. And, when conditions suited him, Derek Underwood, who was not nicknamed 'Deadly' for nothing.

TUFFERS How do you separate Warne and Muralitharan? I mean, I was all right but it was tough playing in the same era as the two greatest spinners the game has ever seen. You always felt team-mates were judging you against those two – a guaranteed lose–lose situation. Like I was the pop-gun and they were the heavy artillery.

ISA Shane Warne. Even in the 2005 men's Ashes, when he wasn't at his best, he took 40 wickets to become the all-time greatest Ashes wicket-taker. He never lost his inner belief.

EBONY It's between Warne and Muralitharan. Warne created so much magic and Murali had this air of mystery. Narrowly, I'd go for Shane because he has an incredible force of character.

CARLOS Bangladesh's Shakib Al Hasan. Never could work him out. Enough said.

ALISON For England, Graeme Swann. He bowled with passion and personality as well as skill, and was instrumental in that famous 2010–11 Ashes win Down Under. Outside England, Shane Warne. He was the archetypal surfer dude with his bleached blond hair and bad-boy image but he could rip a cricket ball like no-one else. He got wickets as much through force of character and reputation as his talent and skill. He would always delight in announcing a new specialist delivery he'd apparently invented just before an Ashes series.

AATIF Muttiah Muralitharan. Obvious answer but those popping-out eyes, strange expression and odd noises would do for me. And that's before the ball has even left his hand.

CHAPTER 5

FANTASY *TMS* – ON DEBUT

〰〰〰〰〰〰〰〰〰〰〰〰〰〰〰〰〰〰〰〰〰〰〰〰〰〰〰〰〰〰

In which Aggers and Tuffers cast a
commentator's eye over their respective
England debuts.

AGGERS

Tuffers and I couldn't resist this. If only we could have been in the commentary box to assess each other's – and our own – England debuts. Here we speculate on what we *might* have said at the Oval in 1984 and the Melbourne Cricket Ground in 1990.

AGGERS – 5TH TEST, THE OVAL, ENGLAND V. WEST INDIES, 9–14 AUGUST 1984

Making an international debut is a career-defining moment for professional cricketers. Who wouldn't want to come into a side brimming with confidence, packed with experience and fired with momentum from earlier victories? And who wouldn't want opposition that's struggling for form and unsure of its position on the world stage. Unfortunately for me, the new boy in an England team facing the West Indies for the final home Test of 1984, the above 'wants' were noticeably absent. England had lost the previous four matches of the series, although 'lost' doesn't tell the half of it. We had been annihilated, losing by an innings and 180 runs in the 1st Test, nine wickets in the 2nd, eight wickets in the 3rd, and an innings and 64 runs in the 4th. We had batting experience and class in David Gower and Allan Lamb and, of course, we had Ian Botham. But Botham couldn't keep bailing out a team whose top-order batting looked flaky and whose bowling attack was underpowered.

Against lesser opposition we might have got away with it. But that West Indies Test team was probably the greatest ever seen. Not only that, it was performing in all its swaggering pomp. There were

destructive batsmen like Gordon Greenidge, Desmond Haynes, Viv
Richards and captain Clive Lloyd, and a fearsome fast-bowling attack
which could rotate Malcolm Marshall, Michael Holding, Joel Garner
and Eldine Baptiste. Michael Holding was spot on when he later
observed that they 'hammered everyone'. So it was into this cricketing
ordeal by fire that I nervously wandered out to mark my run.

Dad was there and he got very emotional. He'd missed my county
debut but now he was watching me play for England. He never
could have imagined that when he was teaching me how to bowl
back home in our garden. And it all started so well. Lloyd won the
toss and opted to bat and, although I didn't claim a wicket in that
first innings, the tourists were at one point reduced to 70 for 6, with
Botham finishing on 5–72 to become the first all-rounder to hit the
magic triple of 3000 Test runs and 300 wickets. Lloyd's 60 later
ensured some respectability but the Windies 190 total was well
below par. Unfortunately, we succumbed to 162 in reply and in their
second innings the tourists smashed 346 thanks to a Haynes century.
For me, there was at least some personal satisfaction because my
first two Test wickets were as big as they come.

First, I had Gordon Greenidge caught at slip, and that brought Viv
Richards to the crease. Viv was, of course, Ian Botham's close pal
and Beefy immediately came over with instructions to 'give him
nothing pitched up until I give you the signal'. I duly obliged for four
overs, got the signal, pitched one up and had Viv lbw. A bit high, a bit
leggy but David Constant gave it. Viv always insists he would have
reviewed it if the technology had been around then. I tell him I
would have got Umpire's Call. Whatever, dismissing two of the

greatest batsmen the game has seen was a big thing, although it wasn't enough. Needing 375 to win, we lost by 172 runs and the West Indies claimed their 5–0 series 'Blackwash' – the only time a visiting team has won every Test match of an England tour. It was their eighth Test triumph on the bounce and they would go on to post a record 11 consecutive victories. Indeed, between 1980 and 1994–5, they were undefeated in 29 successive Test series – almost double the next longest sequence of 16 by Australia between 2001 and 2004–5.

I felt I'd done OK under the circumstances. Yet – and this is not a whinge or a moan – I never truly felt a part of that England side. I didn't know half of them and I never had the confidence in myself to think I was good enough, that I rightfully belonged, even though I got those two at the Oval. It was the same right through my brief time with England. The game that followed, a one-off Test against Sri Lanka at Lord's, was another tough one. It was a beautiful day, a flat pitch and a very short boundary. Gower put them in and to this day I'll never know why – I'm sure he doesn't either – and it was horrendous. One by one our bowlers broke down, Sidath Wettimuny flayed us for 190 and they were well over 400 for 4 by the end of the second day. I bowled Arjuna Ranatunga and also got Aravinda de Silva, so I got good people out. But it came at a price.

Looking back, my selection for England was almost too much of a dream come true. When Ollie Robinson was asked after his debut whether Test cricket had come too early he replied: 'No, I was ready two years ago.' That was the opposite of my approach. I almost felt I should really be back at home, watching the game on a black-and-white telly, curtains drawn, munching one of Mum's sandwiches.

AGGERS ON AGGERS

Agnew looks like he's pinching himself to make sure he's actually playing for England rather than dreaming about it. It's a tough challenge to come in at this stage of a series. His team-mates' morale seems shot to pieces. They're trying their best but they know they've been outgunned, they've seen colleagues struck and hurt by these fast bowlers, and frankly they all look knackered. Agnew is obviously inexperienced, still only 24, but that said, he's got pace, which always troubles batsmen and is something England have been seeking. From what I've seen of him as a tail-ender, though, he won't fancy facing the West Indies pace attack.

TUFFERS ON AGGERS

Well, now steaming in again is this tall, gangly, young quick with his dreadful mullet haircut. He's so thin it must be hard for the batters to spot him as he runs in but he can swing the ball both ways with amazing control, he can wobble the seam and in Gordon Greenidge and Viv Richards he's just got the scalps of two of the greatest attacking Test batsmen the game has ever seen. Mind you, that ball that got Viv lbw? Surely, it had to be missing leg?

TUFFERS – 2ND TEST, MELBOURNE CRICKET GROUND, AUSTRALIA V. ENGLAND, 26–30 DECEMBER 1990

The Aussies went into this series in a thoroughly chipper mood after winning the Ashes in England two years earlier and securing home series wins against Sri Lanka and Pakistan. But the way we snatched the 1986–7 Ashes in Australia still rankled and their skipper Allan Border was determined it wouldn't happen again. He got an early boost when our captain Graham Gooch pulled out of the 1st Test with an injured finger, leaving Michael Atherton and Wayne Larkins to open the batting. Yet we were generally in good spirts. We had just beaten India and New Zealand in home Test series and we'd looked promising during warm-up matches. However, that 1st Test at the Gabba in Brisbane proved a wake-up call. Put into bat, we struggled to 194 with only David Gower contributing a meaningful total. There was brief optimism when Australia also faffed around to fall 42 runs short, but then our second innings was even worse, ending on 114, and Aussie openers Mark Taylor and Geoff Marsh knocked off the required runs undefeated.

I'd been left out of that match but made my debut in the 2nd Test at Melbourne in an attack which included my old Middlesex mucker

Angus Fraser, all-rounder Phil DeFreitas and the extremely quick Devon Malcolm. Gooch, now fully recovered, won the toss and batted, and we hit a competitive 352 thanks to a Gower century, 79 from Alec Stewart and 64 from Larkins. Australia again fell 40-odd short but again it didn't matter. In the second innings, we lost six wickets inside 50 minutes courtesy of a rampant Bruce Reid. Mike Atherton, who had a miserable match, scoring 0 and 4, later cited 'general incompetence' as the main reason for the collapse, although he also highlighted an issue in which certain players resented Gooch's no-nonsense, hard-work ethic, which was at odds with previous skipper Gower's more relaxed approach to training.

Australia eventually cruised through their second innings despite losing two wickets with just 10 on the board at close of play on day four and 187 still required. Rodney Marsh again delivered while David Boon carried his bat for a bullying 94. The Boon innings still gives me nightmares. We'd talked ourselves into thinking we might have a chance in the match and a third cheap wicket would definitely have given us the momentum. I'd started my spell and midway through an over I asked the umpire, Peter McConnell, how many balls were left. That was a habit of mine, especially when I was nervous. Without even a glance he replied: 'Count 'em yourself, you Pommie bastard.' I couldn't believe what I'd heard. I told him I wasn't having that, a ding-dong started between us and then Gooch, hearing what was unfolding, hot-footed over to start a ding-dong of his own. 'Excuse me, umpire,' said Graham. 'You can't talk to my players like that.' In that moment, I saw him in a new light.

McConnell clearly felt he had to show who was boss because, a few overs later, I fired in a short, wide, ball which Boon tried to cut away. Instead, he got a massive nick to Jack Russell behind the stumps and off I went, charging down the wicket, barely bothering to appeal, madly celebrating my first Test wicket. Boon stayed put as he was entitled to do. I turned to the umpire who, smiling broadly, stared me straight in the eye and said: 'Not out.' To which I replied, 'You f***ing bastard.'

The Aussies never did lose another wicket and the result was that I got in all the papers for throwing a tantrum. Even my father gave me an earful: 'Bloody hell, boy, what have you done now? Keep your mouth shut. It's your first Test, don't start causing trouble by having a pop at the umpire.' I just thought: 'Welcome to Australia, Phil.'

McConnell seemed to follow us everywhere on that tour. You've got to take 20 wickets to win a Test but it sometimes felt like we needed 40. Some of the umpiring decisions, particularly in Australia and India, at that time were ridiculous. Even the immaculate Alec Stewart got fined at Sydney when an Aussie batter got a deafening inside edge on to his pad and was caught at fine leg. The umpire ruled not out and Stewie hurled the ball to the ground in disbelief. So I certainly wasn't the only England Test player guilty of occasional dissent. Australia eventually secured a 3–0 series win, although it should be said that we fought well in the final three Tests and could even have swung a couple our way. At Sydney, I even managed to taste a little sweet revenge, finishing with 5–61 in a haul which included, satisfyingly, the wicket of one David Boon.

TUFFERS ON TUFFERS

Tufnell seems to have landed in Test cricket with a particularly feisty attitude towards the umpires. Words were exchanged with Peter McConnell during his first over in this Australian innings and now it looks like he has again got the hump with McConnell over that last delivery to David Boon. Tufnell seems convinced Boon was caught behind. He's not happy with McConnell and the England captain Graham Gooch has had to intervene to calm things down. But the umpire's decision isn't going to change.

AGGERS ON TUFFERS

We're almost at the end of the fourth day in Melbourne. Australia are already two wickets down in their second innings and although that 197 target is gettable the match would be finely balanced with another wicket now. There's a lot on Phil Tufnell's shoulders – this is his debut Test and on a wearing pitch he'll be expected to get turn – but he took 65 first-class wickets in England over the summer and he may cause the Aussies some problems. Here he is, bowling to David Boon, a wide-ish delivery, Boon shapes to cut . . . there's a huge appeal, Tufnell goes charging off down the wicket, he's convinced Boon has been caught behind by Jack Russell. And yet umpire Peter McConnell is unmoved. Tufnell looks livid. A few moments ago, he was having an intense argument about something with McConnell and the England captain had to intervene. This decision isn't going to calm things down. But whatever, Boon survives.

TOP LIST

Captain I'd most like to have played for

AGGERS Andrew Strauss had huge respect from those he led, and playing under Steve Waugh must have been an interesting experience. I think Shane Warne would have been a brilliant tactical Test captain.

TUFFERS At Test level, Mike Gatting would have been my ideal captain. He had a sense of fun, was good at keeping a dressing room calm and understood that players were all different. He would have particularly understood how to deal with a gobby kid like me.

ISA Probably Shane Warne. I like his cricket mindset – basically that you're never out of a game. He's an astute thinker but he's also the type who would take a gamble based on instinct. I've always loved that in a captain.

EBONY Virat Kohli. Not particularly Kohli the player but definitely Kohli the leader. His attitude to the game, his will to win, his amazing facial expressions – I reckon players feed off his energy.

CARLOS There's three I can't separate: Rahul Dravid because he's my absolute idol and I had the privilege of being coached by him; Mahendra Singh Dhoni, because everyone who has played under him has only good things to say; and Viv Richards because he was so brazen, so aggressive, and the fact that he mentored one of the teams I captained. Viv made you feel you could punch through mountains.

AATIF I'd love to say Babar Azam although he's not quite there yet. Then there's Misbah-ul-Haq, who transformed Pakistani cricket. But it has to be Michael Vaughan, especially in 2005 when his England team was ruthless. Nasser Hussain re-ignited England's spark after they fizzled to an all-time-low in the 'nineties but Michael turned them into a truly formidable force. As a captain, he never ran out of plans.

CHAPTER 6

TMS DOWN UNDER

◇◇◇

In which Tuffers throws a tantrum
and helps Aggers bag a new job.

THE ASHES, 1990–1

AGGERS

For Tuffers and myself, 1990 was a landmark year for very different reasons. For me, it was the end of an era, my final season as a professional cricketer; for Tuffers, things were just getting interesting. As I prepared to venture cautiously into the world of tabloid newspapers, he was packing his case for Australia as an England debutant fighting for the Ashes. And it just so happened that these twists of fate threw us together Down Under.

In the early spring of that year I was playing for Leicestershire at Chelmsford when the *Today* sports editor Mike Crouch rang saying he wanted me to be his full-time staff correspondent for the 1990–1 Ashes tour. I'd been doing occasional articles for Mike, which had provided some experience of working with tabloid journalists – otherwise known as the Beastie Boys – but it was still a big punt on me. I knew that some old-school writers wouldn't want me there. They could see that more and more cricketers would be taking their jobs and, although there would be no unpleasantness, I suspected I might be frozen out. But signing for *Today* was great for me. Rolling news was coming in, there was a much sharper approach to sports coverage and working alongside experienced reporters meant I had to learn fast.

I brought my whites and boots along for the Australian tour and at Brisbane, my first Test match as a cricket correspondent, I got a phone message from the England team manager Micky Stewart asking if I could bowl at a nets practice session ahead of the 1st Test, due to start on 23 November. The *Guardian*'s Mike Selvey, who was really the first professional cricketer turned correspondent, had cautioned me against this kind of thing on the basis that you couldn't be both inside and outside the England camp. He warned I would 'get nabbed'. But I ignored him and duly turned up.

Graham Gooch was suffering from a bad finger infection picked up in a practice game and, as Allan Lamb was deputising as captain, I asked the tour manager Peter Lush if I could interview Allan. I was told he had too much on and that no-one else was available. This seemed a bit unfair given that I'd come to help the team so when Peter pointed me to a net it seemed a good opportunity to prove to my new media colleagues that I was on their side. I told him I couldn't do it if he wasn't going to help us in return. Pretty soon, still in my whites, I was surrounded by tabloid hacks offering their support. I think the headline in the *Sun* next day was, 'Agnew Tells England to Get Stuffed', which was somewhat ironic, given that I'd only tried to stand up for the press. But it did rather prove Mike Selvey's point. In fact, I later went round to Robin Smith's hotel room to get his views on the deputy captain. Robin told me he was unaware of any press blackout and happily gave me an interview.

The 1st Test ended in an ignominious ten-wicket defeat for England. Our batting was blown away by Terry Alderman, who took 6–47 in the second innings and skittled us for 114. But the Ashes were then put on hold for a month while attention switched to the World Series Cup, a one-day tournament between Australia, New Zealand

and England. England's management wanted to give Tuffers some practice against fast bowling so in Perth they lined up a bunch of young, keen Aussies to bomb him in the nets. The aim was to get him ready for his first World Series match against New Zealand on 7 December but things did not go to plan and the resulting 'Tuffers Tantrum', as it became known, would bizarrely have a major influence on my own media prospects.

And this was a proper tantrum. Phil thought that exposing him to continuous fast bowling was a ridiculous idea which was going to end in him possibly getting seriously injured. He was probably right. Net surfaces weren't always reliable and, after all, he wasn't in the team to flay deliveries from Aussie pacemen. He threw his bat away, unleashed a volley of vibrant language and very publicly stomped off. However, unlike some of my press colleagues, I missed it all because I had just filed a thoughtfully crafted piece on Terry Alderman's plans for getting Graham Gooch out. The tabloids all went with the Tuffers story and when their back pages landed on the *Today* sports desk, my article was binned and a rewritten version of the 'Tuffers Tantrum' was substituted with my name on it. It was a better tabloid story but I was absolutely livid and this happened to coincide with *TMS* producer Peter Baxter approaching me about the BBC cricket correspondent job. I'd already said a polite 'no' to Peter but the Tuffers episode changed my mind. I'd also had the *Independent*'s correspondent Martin Johnson, a good friend, in my ear saying I was bonkers to turn the BBC down and what the hell did I think I was doing. For years, I don't think Phil realised the impact his tantrum had on my career.

TUFFERS

Aggers is right about that because, until we started putting this book together, I had no idea that I'd unwittingly steered him into the arms of the Beeb. I remember the incident very well though. Micky Stewart had bunged a few quid at some First Grade bowlers to come and give our lower order some batting practice. Fair enough, but all I could think about was the nets at Perth being like greased lightning. I can still remember putting my pads on and thinking, 'Bloody hell,' when there's this deafening, throbbing noise and two blokes on Harley-Davidson bikes pull into the practice area. They turned out to be brothers who used to open the bowling for Eastern Suburbs or somewhere. They had on all this leather gear and appeared to be Hells Angels practising impersonations of Arnold Schwarzenegger's Terminator. Their massive Merv Hughes-style moustaches further complemented the look they were going for.

As the first balls came down, it was like they were playing Kill-A-Pom. One got me in the chest pad, another whooshed past my nose and the fourth hit the glove in front of my face with both my feet off the floor. At which point I shouted, 'This is f***ing stupid,' and stormed out of the nets swearing at them – I may have called them Aussie twats – and swinging my bat in their direction. They then accused me of being a lily-livered Pommie bastard. Micky intervened with, 'Get back in the nets, Tuffers,' but I headed off to the hotel shouting back: 'Micky, you're joking, they're trying to kill me.' It was quite an incident and I'm not surprised it made the papers. It was also entirely unnecessary because, as it turned out, I didn't need to bat against New Zealand and we won that game comfortably.

Perth was one of only two batting nets I ever had with England. The other one was much later in my career at Johannesburg in 1999 when Duncan Fletcher found me hiding in the toilets and insisted I practise against Alex Tudor. He stood over me while I put my pads on and then walked me over to the nets like he was my security guard, which in a way he was. The sightscreen was broken so I whispered to Tudes that a few gentle half-volleys would be acceptable. First ball, he came steaming in with a full delivery which unfortunately for me was the perfect in-swinging yorker. I couldn't see it because it had come out of a forest background, it smashed me on the big toe and then demolished my stumps. This time I'm hopping out of the nets once again, accusing my coach of trying to kill me. So my stats on England batting nets reads: 2–5–5–2. Or, put another way, did two, faced five, missed five, retired hurt twice.

AGGERS

The next Ashes Test was due to start in Melbourne on Boxing Day. A four-day warm-up game had been arranged at Ballarat, a former gold-prospecting town in Victoria, and with *Today*'s permission I was covering it for BBC Radio. This was a favour to *TMS* producer Peter Baxter, who had gone home for Christmas, and also a chance to showcase my broadcasting skills to the BBC who, I now hoped, would be my future employer. However, I immediately discovered to my horror that my seat was bang in the middle of the newspaper reporters' section.

I hate broadcasting from a press box but if we haven't got the rights to a match it's what you have to do. I'm not comfortable with it even now. It's easy to mess up a live 30-second take and you feel everyone's listening even though they're probably not and wouldn't give a stuff anyway. Fortunately, an Australian telecoms engineer was hanging around and, on hearing of my dilemma, pointed towards 'the groundsman's hut' – effectively a garden shed – and insisted: 'No worries, mate, we'll put you in there.' He then unwound a mega-extension cable to connect press box and shed, draping it over a large tree which stood in the way.

This all seemed quite agreeable until I opened the shed on my first morning to find a fearsome Alsatian dog baring his teeth and snarling ominously. He belonged to the groundsman and neither of them were too happy about giving up their hut and kennel to the BBC. We eventually reached a compromise in which the dog would be removed whenever I arrived to broadcast one of my regular updates. But he was forever pawing at the door and I'm sure listeners could hear the occasional background bark.

TUFFERS

From Ballarat we went straight into the 2nd Ashes Test and my colourful England debut, covered extensively in the previous chapter. Then it was back to the World Series and a New Year's Day appointment with Australia at Sydney. The match provided another opportunity for me to be at the centre of an on-field drama, although this time it was entirely my own fault. Mark and Steve Waugh were batting together, Australia were in trouble at 82 for 4 and another wicket would have given us a clear edge. When Mark Waugh nicked a shot to backward point his brother Steve called for the run and set off only to see Eddie Hemmings pounce on the ball and throw it to me at the bowler's end. Here was a great chance to run Steve out because Mark hadn't moved and both of them were stranded at the striker's end. All I needed to do was catch the ball and break the stumps. Convinced he was a goner, Steve began walking towards the pavilion, but then the ball bounced off my hands like they were a pair of frying pans and he realised he might be able to get back in his crease. Even then, I had time to pick up the ball and run over to dislodge the bails but, instead, for some unaccountable reason, I aimed a throw at the stumps. I missed, Steve got home, and the 65,000 crowd rose as one in sheer glee. The noise was unbelievable.

For much of the remainder of the game the TV director repeatedly replayed my shame on the big screen and, for the first time in my professional cricket career, I sensed my lower lip wobbling. It was horrific but at least I did get Steve out a couple of overs later and finished with 3-40 off my ten overs. But it wasn't enough to prevent Australia cruising to a 68-run win and all but end England's interest in the competition.

AGGERS

It was an unbelievably horrible moment, an absolute stinker. It was on a par with Nathan Lyon's nightmare in the 3rd Ashes Test at Headingley in 2019 when it seemed so simple for Nathan to run out Jack Leach and win the game. Yet he couldn't manage it. The Tuffers blunder was perhaps slightly worse because, after he failed to catch the ball, he grabbed it and, with a great flourish, then tried and failed to throw down the stumps from point-blank range. I really do wish I'd been commentating on that.

We stayed in Sydney for the 3rd Test and when that ended in a draw Australia were two up with two to play, which meant they retained the Ashes. But the series could still be squared, there was pride at stake and no England–Australia game ever lacks meaning. So there was plenty for the players to prove as we headed north for a tour match against Queensland at Carrara. I was there for the *Today* newspaper sitting alongside Christopher Martin-Jenkins, then still BBC cricket correspondent. By the morning of the third day, England were well in charge, John Morris and Robin Smith had both got centuries, but then Morris got out and Gower followed cheaply soon afterwards. An hour or so after Gower walked off, we suddenly saw these two vintage biplanes roaring in low over the stadium, wiggling their wings, whereupon everyone – apart from CMJ, who just hurrumphed and muttered a lot about noisy blessed planes – rose to clap and cheer. We obviously had no idea who was up there and I completely forgot about it until my photographer, a sports specialist called Adrian Murrell, wandered over later that afternoon and said: 'We've got a good story here, mate. That was Gower and Morris in those Tiger Moths and I've got the photos to prove it.'

I congratulated him and agreed that we'd got a big tabloid exclusive if we could only keep it quiet. Sadly, word leaked out and soon the whole press pack was on the case. It led to a hilarious press conference at the end of the day in which the daring duo's exploits were put to a blissfully unaware England captain, Graham Gooch, and the tour manager, Peter Lush. They, together with England coach Micky Stewart, stomped off in a right old temper to find the culprits but, with no little chutzpah, the pair had already gone back to the airfield to sit in a cockpit so that another photographer could snap photos of them. Not only that, it emerged that Gower had got an advance sub out of his tour expenses to pay for the flight and that Peter Lush had therefore financed it, albeit unwittingly. Our team hotel had an open reception area and I have this clear memory of Micky and Peter lying in wait for David and John, and pouncing on them as they came waltzing back from the airfield. Everyone eventually saw the funny side, except Graham Gooch. It ruined his and David's friendship and I don't believe they ever got that back.

TUFFERS

It was quite an edgy jape because if we'd suffered a sudden batting collapse at the point Gower and Morris dipped out we might have taken the field two men short like some village side struggling to find players. I'd been vaguely aware of Gower hatching plans for a flying escapade but I didn't take much notice until those Tiger Moths came rumbling in, dive-bombing the ground, and I saw Judgie (Robin Smith) and Allan Lamb out on the pitch pointing bat handles to the sky and pretending to shoot them down. Both knew what was going on but Micky, Goochie and Peter Lush had no idea it was England's No. 4 and No. 6 up there because the pair of them were togged up in Biggles caps and goggles. So all three cheered and clapped along with the rest. Gower and Morris arrived back just as I was bowled out and scuttled into the back of the pavilion looking like a pair of reverse-colour pandas – white where the goggles had been; sooty from engine smoke everywhere else. They had a wash and brush up, got their whites on and carried on without the tour management suspecting a thing.

Until the after-match press conference, that is. Micky Stewart and Goochie were asked about the fly-past and gave the full PR number; how it was a wonderful sight, very patriotic, etc. But then the next question: How did they feel about Gower and Morris flying Tiger Moths while playing in a match? At which point faces turned distinctly stony, the press conference was halted and as they stormed out through the swing doors all you could hear was Micky shouting: 'Where the f***'s Gower?' Someone then attempted a weak cover-up by telling him Gower and Morris had gone for a run. Which, knowing David, was vanishingly unlikely. They had both legged it pronto. I just thought: 'What a blast it is touring with England. A few lagers every day, a nice wander around Australia, boys off having a jaunt in pre-war biplanes. This is the life.' In fact, Carrara is full of happy memories for me because I got a five-for to help us win the match.

NICE LINE
The Tigers that came to tea

Before heading off on their flight of fancy, David Gower and John Morris had every reason to believe they were in the England management's good books. Although Gower had succumbed for just 13 in the Queensland game, he had banked typically stylish centuries in both the 2nd and 3rd Tests. And while Morris had not yet appeared in the Test team his contribution at Carrara had been an excellent 132. The problem would be Graham Gooch's disciplinarian style of captaincy, as Gower knew all too well. When he and Morris were finally tracked down and hauled before the fines committee of Gooch, Stewart and Lush, the atmosphere was several degrees below frosty. Gower, as senior pro, tried a conciliatory approach by suggesting the management could 'either be heavy about it or . . . treat it as a harmless prank'. Unsurprisingly, they picked Option 1. 'Gooch and Stewart were very regimental in their dealings at the time,' he said later. 'It was a one-rule-for-all-types regime which didn't allow someone to have a little bit of fun.'

Sentence was not pronounced until the eve of the 4th Test. By all accounts the disciplinary panel had considered sending the pair home but given the tourists' parlous position in the series – two down with two to play – it was felt Gower's runs and experience could not be so easily jettisoned. Instead, both players were hit with £1000 fines – a sum Gower dryly observed was 'rather steep' for a 20-minute joy ride. Sadly, the whole episode signalled the beginning of the end of his illustrious international career. His next four innings in the Tests at Adelaide and Perth totalled only 55 runs and he made only three further appearances for his country after that. As for Morris, he never played for England again.

AGGERS

The tour ended with a draw at Adelaide and another emphatic Australian win at Perth to give them a 3–0 series win. My abiding memory of the Perth game was the presence of the Barmy Army because this was the first time they'd really got together as a kind of unofficial supporters' club. The airlines had been hit by strike action, making it difficult to get from Adelaide to Perth for the back-to-back last Tests and so some company – Toyota, I think – laid on road transport for the Army, and they travelled the entire 1700-odd miles in convoy before being shepherded into their own reserved area inside the WACA. There were signs up which read, 'Perth Welcomes The Barmy Army', but Australia didn't really know what to do with them because they had never encountered such mass support. Now, of course, the Aussies do all they can to split them up. I'd say 99 per cent of the Barmy Army behaves extremely well – the only grudge I have with them is when they place themselves directly under my microphone and chant as I'm trying to work.

TUFFERS

My regular fielding positions were fine leg and third man, well out of the way, so I spent a lot of time hanging around the boundary. At Perth, there was an archetypal Australia supporter – hat with corks, flip-flops, shorts, a 'Come On Aussie' singlet and an Esky packed with beer. He'd be sat on the bank and the first time I'd walk down there during the day's play he'd smile, nice as pie, offer a 'Good morning, Tuffers', enquire whether I was OK . . . and then spend the next six hours as Evil Aussie hurling dog's abuse my way at every opportunity. Then, when play ended, he'd magically transform back to Nice Aussie: 'See you tomorrow, Tuffers, same time. Sleep well, mate.' Bizarrely we became quite good friends. The Aussie crowd was always in your ear. I'd get told my skipper was signalling me to move to the left but then suddenly it was: 'NO, Tuffers, NO. To the RIGHT.'

It wasn't just the verbals. On the boundary at Auckland I once found myself facing a hail of fruit, including an under-ripe peach which almost knocked me out. In Bulawayo I got de-bagged by one supporter while fielding at fine leg. And in the West Indies people used to throw fags and lighters at me. In fairness, I didn't mind that and I picked them all up. I never liked missing out on a free fag. These were the days when stewards were like hen's teeth – you were basically on your own out in the deep – but on the whole I didn't see cricket crowds as intimidating. Fast bowlers – now *they* were intimidating.

ENGLAND IN NEW ZEALAND, 1992

AGGERS

I'd long been a big admirer of Phil as a bowler and appreciated that
he offered something different. However, my first interview with
him didn't happen until January 1992 in Christchurch, my first tour
as BBC cricket correspondent, when England rattled up 580 for 9
in their first innings and Tuffers took four of New Zealand's top
five wickets to reduce them to 312. He returned figures of
39–10–100–4 – a great effort by any standards – and Gooch duly
enforced the follow-on. Despite this, the match was heading for a
nailed-on draw. At tea on the last day, I'd got my report ready, the
press guys had everything written up, the Black Caps openers had
moved to 81 for 0 and, although Tuffers then got Blair Hartland and
Danny Morrison fell for a duck, New Zealand put on another 100
for the third wicket. Then they collapsed as Phil dismantled the
middle order to set up an amazing finish.

Only Martin Crowe stood in the way, batting sensibly to take time
out of the game, and with New Zealand just four runs behind on
second innings Crowe knew one lusty blow would be enough. There
would be insufficient time for the teams to change around and
England would have no chance of hitting the winning runs. As it

was, in Tuffers own words, Crowe skied a 'floaty ball-on-a-string delivery', which Derek Pringle duly pouched to give England victory and Tuffers second innings figures of 7–47. I was broadcasting for Radio 4's *Today* programme anchored by John Humphrys and found Phil round the back of the pavilion puffing hard on a cigarette. He agreed to an interview and my first question was: 'Well, Phil, that was an extraordinary performance. The New Zealanders had no idea how to play you.' With a live radio audience agog for his analytical views he replied simply: 'Nah, mate. They was shittin' theirselves.' And so it was quickly back to you in the studio, John.

TUFFERS

It was like I was bowling hand grenades at them. It was a phenomenal hour of cricket and it was special because absolutely nobody, not the press, not the players on either side, saw it coming. If Martin Crowe had hit one more ball for four the game would have been drawn and we'd have headed back to the hotel. All of a sudden, the players I'd always looked up to, the likes of Allan Lamb and Robin Smith, were pouring me champagne and giving me a cuddle in the dressing room. Up to that point, I think they weren't sure whether I was any good or not so it was a big moment in my career. I still think that Aggers interview with me afterwards must be the shortest ever broadcast live on the *Today* programme.

You need to remember days like that because you sure as hell won't forget the bad ones. One of my worst came during our 1997 tour to New Zealand when Nathan Astle and Danny 'The Duckman' Morrison defied us for two-and-a-half hours during the 1997 1st Test in Auckland, ensuring New Zealand earned a draw. They had an unbeaten 106-run partnership, of which Danny scored 14. It was a dead pitch but failing to get out the worst tail-ender in the world at the time – Morrison recorded 24 ducks during his 48 Test matches – was a bit of a downer. Especially as I felt it was my job to remove him. Afterwards, I barely spoke for two days.

THE ASHES, 1994–5

TUFFERS

Another Ashes tour; another shedload of emotional baggage taken along. I was going through a tough time, what with everything happening back home – an acrimonious divorce, dealing with solicitors, people effectively stealing things from my house – and I'd tried to keep all this under wraps. My whole life was up in the air. It occurred to me before the tour started that I wasn't in the right frame of mind and I mentioned this to my dad. He told me he was sorry about the divorce but that I shouldn't let it get in the way of my career and the honour of playing for England in an Ashes series. The divorce would work itself out but I might never get another opportunity. So I should get my arse on the plane and go for it. And I agreed. I thought: 'Pull yourself together, Tufnell.' In reality, I had what would now be called a mental health issue.

Looking back on what happened to me in Australia, it is in one sense quite funny. But at the time it wasn't and it's absolutely right that everyone's mental health is taken much more seriously these days. While it's a privilege to play professional sport it doesn't mean you're inured from the stress it places on you or the fact that you can be away from friends and family for long periods. I would never underestimate the effect of pressure to succeed alongside a feeling of isolation.

Anyway, one night in Perth it all got too much and by 2 a.m. I was storming around my hotel, crying, shouting and chucking things around including the telly and various bedside lights. I'd been on the phone all day trying to sort out the kids, the divorce settlement, the solicitors, and nothing was clear in my mind. My behaviour understandably unnerved my room-mate Phil DeFreitas, who locked himself in the bog and called tour management saying: 'Send help, Phil's having a moment.' Next thing, there's a knock on the door and I find myself facing M. J. K. Smith, the tour manager, and a couple of blokes in white coats. I honestly thought they were cricket umpires, which gives you some idea how confused I was.

A short tussle followed during which they restrained me, bundled me down the fire escape, pushed me into the back of an unmarked van and drove off to what I later learned was a psychiatric hospital. I was getting more and more emotional, still unsure what was happening, wondering what Dad would think, worrying about being sent home, the shame, the this and the that. On arrival, I was led into this room where a doctor removed the straitjacket, shone a light in my eyes, put me in a gown tied loosely up the back and started asking about my childhood. That rather snapped my brain back into action and I worked out what was happening. As soon as a nurse went off to get me a coffee, leaving me alone, I legged it.

I dashed down the corridor barefoot, past the receptionists, oblivious to shouts that I was escaping, and sprinted through the double doors into the Perth night. The orderlies were chasing me and I was hurdling fences and trampling across suburban gardens to try and throw them off. Eventually, I found an open garden shed and hid in there to let things calm down while I thought what to do. When I couldn't see any more flashing torches I decided I'd get myself back to the hotel somehow and started walking down the road in my gown, arse hanging out the back, houses all in darkness, not a soul around, hoping to wave down the first car I saw. And thankfully it was a taxi driver heading into Perth for an early morning shift. I stumbled into the road, arms flailing, whereupon he stopped, wound down the window, looked up at this wild-eyed, gibbering, half-naked bloke and said: 'G'day, Tuffers. Been in a spot of trouble? Jump in, mate.'

At the hotel, I had a beer and smoke and then decided to alert someone from the tour management team to the fact that I was back. On the off-chance, I tried our team room, still in my hospital gown, to find Athers and the rest of them in an absolute flap working out how to get Ian Salisbury over from Sussex or Min Patel from Kent. I couldn't think what to say so I just vaguely waved my beer can and fag at them and said: 'A'right lads? What time's the bus tomorrow?' There was utter silence, all these faces open-mouthed, so I followed up with, 'Sorry about all this. Hopefully we can just move on,' and then walked out without a further word being said, giving them a final flash of my arse. I got my head down, set an alarm and was on the bus at 8.30 a.m. sharp, apologising to everyone again, saying I was looking forward to a good practice, which didn't sound too credible.

Looking back, I'm not too happy about being fined £2000 for what was essentially a cry for help but, truth is, the management didn't know what to do and neither did I. In a funny kind of way, they handled it quite well because by simply getting on with the tour they ensured I didn't dwell on stuff at home and pulled myself together. But, no question, if something like that happened these days it would be handled very differently. We should all be thankful for that.

THE ASHES, 2006–7, AND THE WORLD CUP, 2007

AGGERS

It was going to be Flintoff or Strauss as captain for the Ashes. Strauss was in and out of the side but, more importantly, Flintoff had done great work as England captain on the previous winter's tour to India, where he'd had to step up following Michael Vaughan's knee injury. He'd led England charismatically, they'd won the Test match in Bombay against all odds and I felt Freddie deserved the right to step in again for Australia. He got the job but in hindsight it wasn't a great decision. By his own admission, he was off the rails and didn't really have the authority to take the fight to the Aussies. It was generally an unhappy tour, which got off to the worst possible start with a huge wide from Harmison – the first ball of the 1st Test – and after the massive highs of 2005 England didn't seem to understand how badly Australia were hurting. I'm not saying the tourists took the series lightly but they were certainly screwed into the dirt with that 5–0 whitewash.

It was a bad few months for Fred because soon afterwards he launched himself – literally as it turned out – into the Fredalo affair during the 2007 World Cup in the Caribbean. That tournament saw insipid performances from England, who failed to qualify for the semi-finals and limped through their Super 8 matches. It was an unsatisfactory event generally because the West Indies spurned the chance to reconnect with a sport their people loved, a sport that was part of their culture and one in which they had been historically brilliant. Their administrators got the organisation hopelessly wrong. Supporters weren't allowed to bring their musical instruments into grounds, there were limits on the size of flags, they could only buy bottled water of an approved brand inside the ground. It was frankly all very forgettable.

NICE LINE
The Fredalo affair at the 2007 World Cup

The 2006–7 Ashes debacle had been a PR nightmare for the England and Wales Cricket Board (ECB) amid reports of an ingrained drinking culture within the squad. Flintoff reportedly received three warnings over his behaviour on the tour so his decision to head out on a bender with team-mates in St Lucia a few weeks later was particularly ill-advised. Especially as this immediately followed England's abject performance against New Zealand in their opening game of the 2007 World Cup.

The players' night out ended with Freddie attempting to manoeuvre a quayside pedalo in choppy waters – an enterprise dubbed 'The Fredalo Affair' by the tabloids. This ended with the pedalo partially submerged and the England all-rounder assisted to shore by hotel staff. Years later, he conceded it was not his finest hour. 'It was a real low point,' he said. 'I had this press conference and walked across the hotel reception and the England fans, who were only months previously cheering my name and high-fiving me, were shaking their heads. I couldn't make eye contact with them and I thought: "This isn't good." ' Aggers was at the press conference and remembers trying to think of a disarming opening gambit for his TV interview with Flintoff. 'It was all so humiliating for him. I started with: "Andrew, what have you done?" He looked straight back and said: "I've been a very naughty boy", which was a great response for telly.'

THE ASHES, 2010–11

AGGERS

This was England's first Ashes win in Australia since 1986–7 and it was no coincidence that I enjoyed the tour more than any I'd been on. The 5th Test series decider was at the Sydney Cricket Ground with Michael Clarke named captain in the absence of Ricky Ponting, who had fractured his finger. It was obvious that Michael was Ricky's heir apparent so I was keen to get an exclusive interview and bundled him off to a quiet storeroom somewhere beneath one of the SCG stands. I explained to Clarke that this was a very special room because eight years previously I'd interviewed Steve Waugh here on the eve of his brilliant century against England, a knock which saved Waugh's position as Australia's captain. I pointed to the chair Steve sat on and Michael immediately leapt on it as though a bit of the Waugh magic might rub off on him. Superstition is rife in all sport but this was a forlorn hope. Michael was out for 4 in the first innings as Anderson and Bresnan took seven wickets between them, and then had to watch as Alastair Cook hit 189, Ian Bell 115 and Matt Prior 118 to give England a massive 364-run first innings lead. There was no way back from that and the tourists won by an innings and 83 runs to secure their 3–1 series win.

It was a great feeling, especially after we'd been whitewashed 5–0 in the previous Australian Ashes. For me personally, the best bit of the entire tour getting my wife Emma, who had flown out for the final games, on to the outfield at the Melbourne Cricket Ground a few minutes after England won that 4th Test to go 2–1 up in the series and retain the Ashes. That was really special – probably my favourite day in all the years I've done the *TMS* and BBC cricket correspondent jobs. All that time being away from home and suddenly it felt like I could at last show her what I was doing it for. By the end of that game, even the Aussie security people seemed to have lost heart and she somehow found her way up to the *TMS* commentary box and then out on to the ground with me to listen in on my post-match interviews.

Graeme Swann had been recording everything the England players did during the tour and I became aware of him filming some curious dance move, which was apparently called 'The Sprinkler', on the Melbourne outfield. Graeme uploaded the footage and it took on a life of its own. At some point, I'd promised him that if England won the Ashes – which of course they did in the following Test in Sydney – I would do 'The Sprinkler' and fortunately Emma had insisted I practise in anticipation of an England triumph. So I did that outside the Sydney Opera House and then performed it in front of the SCG Members Pavilion moments after England clinched their series victory. Emma said I looked ridiculous but, in fairness, that was the idea. I don't know what has happened to 'The Sprinkler' since. Hopefully I didn't kill it off.

TOP LIST

Captain I most enjoyed playing for

AGGERS I always enjoyed playing under David Gower because he let you think for yourself.

TUFFERS My old Middlesex captain Mike Gatting. I gave him a hard time occasionally but he had a great sense of humour, knew how to handle players and was good at keeping a dressing room calm. Which, in my case, was vital.

ISA Clare Connor, who was my first England captain. I was the youngest of the group. I felt I had to show respect to more experienced players, not step on toes, embrace the role of newbie and so on. Which was fine but Clare is a great motivator and made it crystal clear that I was playing for England on merit. That I had a right to be in that dressing room. She just made me feel properly welcome. It's different now – youngsters coming into a team are allowed to be themselves – but in my time I felt I was tiptoeing round at first.

EBONY Australian batter Mel Jones. She was my idol, she worked us hard, made us take professional sport seriously – then led the partying after games.

CARLOS Kirk Edwards. He always thought outside the box and made you feel as though you were never under pressure at any phase of a match. Or that your selection was ever in question. His captaincy was basically: leave it to me, I'll make the decisions, you just concentrate on your game. I also loved Winston Reid as a captain because he had a saying that no-one panics until he panics. He was a properly cool and calm customer – widely regarded in Barbados as the best cricketer never to play for the West Indies.

AATIF I thoroughly enjoyed playing under the captaincy of my fellow *TMS* broadcaster Dan Norcross. We batted together at the RAF Cricket Ground in Uxbridge during a charity match for the Lord's Taverners. I pulled two balls to the square leg boundary for four. He walked over to me and said, 'Yes . . . that's good. Keep doing that.' The best captains keep it simple.

CHAPTER 7

TUFFERS ON TOUR

In which Tuffers recalls the good, the bad and the downright hilarious from his nine overseas tours.

INDIA, 1993

TUFFERS

Taking on India in their own backyard is a privilege. It's a cricket-loving nation with fantastic, knowledgeable, friendly supporters. But touring there is a big ask for any team physically, mentally and tactically because it's also a vast country, the heat is intense, the food doesn't always agree with you and the flat pitches make life hard for bowlers. On top of all that, our 1993 series in India was beset with problems off the field, not least the serious civil unrest sparked by religious violence. This at times led to literally thousands of armed guards protecting our practice sessions. Then there was an airline strike over the safety of the air transport network and that meant long, sweltering, packed train journeys. We also managed to suffer a couple of self-inflicted wounds: our selectors somehow failed to pick either David Gower, even though he'd averaged 50 in the previous summer series against Pakistan, or Jack Russell, generally considered our best wicketkeeper. Against this backdrop I had well-documented relationship problems back home and I badly missed my baby daughter. All in all, it was not the ideal preparation.

Unsurprisingly, we lost the 1st Test at Kolkata heavily and that created further pressure for our warm-up game in Visakhapatnam against Rest of India. They had a talented young side – Sachin Tendulkar was making his debut as a first-class captain – and it felt as though Ian Salisbury, John Emburey and myself had been thrown into a spinners' bowl-off to decide who would be picked for the next Test at Chennai. Ian had played at Kolkata so I had to bowl my way back into the side.

The tension didn't ease up when the umpire at my end kept calling me for no-balls. This had never arisen as an issue with my bowling before so either he didn't understand the rule, was plain wrong or just wanted to wind me up. In the end, I placed Mike Atherton at short extra cover to check where my foot was landing and, sure enough, it was landing right on the line. It's pointless to dispute basic decisions like this because no umpire is going to admit he is wrong and as a bowler you have to get on with it. But this guy kept on calling me, which made me feel fractious from the off.

No-one had seen much of Tendulkar but everyone had heard what an amazing prodigy he was. Over a beer on the eve of the game, Clem Driver, our official scorer, mentioned that he'd never been out stumped and in India, with its spin-friendly pitches, that was some achievement even in a short career. The stat stuck with me going into the game. I badly wanted to be the first bowler to have Sachin stumped and that would also have been a nice scalp for our wicketkeeper Richard Blakey, who was on that tour for his batting potential and was about to make his England debut. Blakes had done really well for Yorkshire and it was felt he might eventually replace Alec Stewart, allowing Alec to focus more on his role as a front-line batsman. But it was a controversial pick because the selectors had preferred Blakes over Jack Russell.

When Tendulkar was on around 20, I bowled this beautiful delivery
which lured him down the wicket. He went for a big shot back over
my head and completely missed the ball whereupon I started yelling:
'Stump him, Blakes, stump him.' But Blakes dropped the ball and
Sachin scrambled back to safety. I probably said FFS or something
similar, grabbed my cap from the umpire, who was chuckling away,
and then booted it across the outfield all the way down to fine leg in
a very stroppy, the world's-against-me type of teenage tantrum. For
sure, my cap took one hell of a beating. I still shudder at the
memory but in that moment the missed stumping seemed to
encapsulate everything that was going wrong for us as a team and
for me personally.

The match was drawn and afterwards I was pulled in by the tour
management, quite rightly, and fined £500. There were reports of
shouting and a bottle smashing at the meeting. I don't remember
that but it is entirely plausible. Fortunately, Blakes is a great lad and
was very magnanimous in receiving my apology. He was
disappointed with himself, felt he'd let me down, that it was a sitter
and we should have had Sachin. As much as anything, it was an
explosion of frustration on my part. Bowling most of the day, in
90 degrees or whatever, does affect your judgement.

It's worth pointing out here that you are always more likely to get
fined on tour as opposed to home Tests. When I say 'you', I
obviously mean 'me', but it's true. Simply the weight of days spent
around the same people is enough to make players rebel a bit
whereas a home series is just five days at a time and you can get
away. I got fined for all manner of things on tour – everything from

turning up late for the team bus to wearing the wrong shorts in a warm-up. I used to wander in to see the management and before they could say a word ask simply: 'Cash or cheque?' There was a fining culture around England at that time. I was fined on every tour I went on and in the 1990 Ashes series in Australia every single player got fined – even the likes of Michael Atherton, Alec Stewart and Angus Fraser. The only comforting thing about it was that the cash went on an end-of-tour party so, with a few quid knocking around, at least we got a good piss-up.

Ian Salisbury and myself both played in that 2nd Chennai Test, not that it did either of us much good because India won by an innings and 22 runs. I did get Tendulkar out lbw in the 3rd Test at Mumbai in a four-wicket haul. But it didn't get much better for Blakes who got a duck on debut in the 2nd Test and followed that with scores of 1 and 0 in the 3rd. He never played for England again. As a team we were pretty poor and deserved our 3–0 thrashing.

We thought things couldn't possibly get any worse when we moved on to the Sri Lanka leg of the tour. They had some whizzkid of a spinner called Muttiah Muralitharan but, so what, the pitches were bound to be dead flat and the batters would have a field day. That certainly turned out to be true for Sri Lanka in Colombo during the single Test we played. I was bowling in partnership with John Emburey and when we saw that Sanath Jayasuriya was batting at No. 7 it was dispiriting, to say the least. It suggested Sri Lanka had six other batters at least as good as him, for Chrissake, so it was no great surprise when they rattled up 469 in their first innings. The pitch was indeed flat as a fart with not a smidgeon of turn, and

Embers and myself assured our batters there would be absolutely nothing to fear from any spinner. Not a great call as it turned out. When we batted, this little bloke Murali suddenly started making the ball talk. You could literally hear it fizzing as it came at you. I followed all the rules, got forward to the pitch, high elbow, confident of no bounce, only for the ball to leap up and smack me on the head. I mean, what the f***? Were we playing on a different pitch? Soon afterwards, Murali got me lbw and we went on to lose by five wickets. And people ask why I never liked batting?

One good thing about foreign tours was that I could always catch up on a bit of dressing-room kip once my teams started batting. Unless the boys contrived a top- and middle-order collapse, the chances of me wielding the willow early on were vanishingly small and, besides, as any international athlete will tell you, rest is important. That's especially so on tour in hot countries where the bowler with an open, enquiring mind might have taken advantage of some local hospitality the night before and might need to let that work through the system. Just occasionally, my slumbers caused a bit of a fallout with my skipper and the 1st Test of the 1994 West Indies tour at Sabina Park, Kingston, Jamaica, was a case in point.

This was around the time the England management had started trying to make us look more corporate – same hats, same workout gear, same dress code – and that was probably fair enough because we were a bit raggedy. They didn't want a bunch of unshaven blokes tumbling off the team bus when they were supposed to be looking smart and all facing the right way. We had motivational banners up in the dressing room and there was this idea that the whole squad should be out on the pavilion balcony to show unity and support if our guys were batting. And on that first morning at Sabina Park, Mike Atherton and Alec Stewart certainly needed that support as they faced the combined pace attack of Curtly Ambrose, Courtney Walsh and Kenny Benjamin. I wasn't picked for the game but when Athers came in at lunch to discover I'd been enjoying some shut-eye while he and Alec were suffering a right battering, he went ballistic. Phrases such as 'that's piss-poor, Tuffers' echoed loudly around the pavilion corridors.

I hold my hands up to that. I should have been watching Athers and Stewie defying the might of the West Indies but I would say three things in my defence. Firstly, if in the past England had won a toss and batted, no-one would have told Ian Botham he had to sit and watch the openers. Beefy would be off reading the paper or having a shower or on the phone or something. And I was certainly not the only one in our squad struggling to adapt to this shiny new corporate culture. Secondly, I was not relishing the prospect of watching my team-mates face those bowlers on that wicket and so a leisurely shower followed by a cheeky snooze seemed a much better use of my time. Also, it's possible I might have had a little bit of a night out the previous evening.

Thirdly, I have always been a terrible watcher of cricket. I'd scare our batsmen before they even got out there. I never wanted to see Curtly, Courtney and the rest of those Windies pace bowlers in action – it's horrific – so why would our No. 3 bat want me sitting next to him, loudly declaring, 'F***ing hell, that's quick, he's going to kill someone,' when the poor lad is just trying to focus and stay calm. So I often thought the best thing was for me to stay out of the way. In the end, it didn't much matter whether I gave visible support or not because Kenny Benjamin took 6–66 in our first innings, the West Indies smashed 407 in theirs and then went on to win by eight wickets.

We lost that series 3–1, a fair reflection of the teams and conditions, but my abiding memory of it occasionally surfaces like a recurring nightmare to summon me back to the 5th Test in Antigua and the best batter I ever bowled to; one Brian Charles Lara. I don't make that claim lightly because I also saw plenty of the wonderful Sachin Tendulkar scoring for fun against me and England bowlers generally. But Lara, in that spring of 1994, was on an ability level all his very own. And I had the dubious pleasure of delivering balls for him to hit over two-and-a-half strength-sapping days in Antigua as he posted his then world record individual score of 375.

The moment Brian hit the record-breaking runs the place erupted into an impromptu carnival. The game stopped for half an hour, Gary Sobers strolled on to the pitch, the street-food sellers spilled on to the outfield flogging soup and chicken, Chickie's Disco upped the volume, people began dancing around the boundary and, outside, the entire West Indies came to a juddering halt as the islands took in what he'd achieved. It was the most surreal moment of my time in cricket. Yes, it was a flat pitch and a small ground, but the outfield was covered in lumps of clover so I reckon Brian's 375 would have been 420 on a better surface. He seemed to score in blocks of ten rather than ones and twos.

Even now, a cold chill runs down my back as I picture myself running in to bowl at him. I mean, Christ alive, I can't recall a single chance he gave. We had a decent attack – Chris Lewis, Gus Fraser, Andy Caddick and myself – but we didn't even manage to hit him on the pads. Angus, who hated conceding a run more than any bowler I knew, would be bowling this beautiful line just short of a length and Brian would guide it between second slip and gully. Up the slips would go – 'Well bowled, Frase, well bowled, you'll get him soon.' Over time, a *very* long time, it dawned on us that he was playing that shot deliberately. I suggested Gus move a slip to second gully to try and stop it. Brian just angled the bat slightly to score through the gap it left. I think it was as he passed 250 that we finally realised he was taking the piss. You hear plenty of batsmen telling you how they carefully place their shots but bollocks to all that. They see a half volley and they hit it vaguely in the direction of a gap. But Brian? He could hit the ball into a teacup on the boundary.

In the end, you almost become immune to it as the fielding side. I was a pretty feisty bowler on my day but I stopped having a go at him once he nosed above 300 because it sounded a tad hollow to call him a lucky sod. As a spinner, you know a good ball as soon as it's left your hand. A few times I thought: 'That's a beaut. That'll hit the rough patch outside off. That'll give him trouble.' But no. He would just nip back on to his stumps and dispatch it for four. To which the only response was: 'Fecking hell. That's a good shot.' And I almost started enjoying it. It's fair to say that Lara's name is lasered into my psyche because, after I retired, I hosted a group of fans travelling out for the 4th Test of England's 2004 West Indies tour. In that, Brian scored 400 not out. So in two West Indies v. England Tests, I'd watched him score 775 for 1. Pretty much effortlessly.

NICE LINE

Dropping Brian Lara

No cricketer likes dropping catches. If it happens, the hope is that the batter will provide another chance, quickly, to spare the blushes. Unfortunately for wicketkeeper Chris Scott, the player he dropped one June afternoon in 1994 was none other than Brian Lara, the West Indian legend who only two months earlier had posted his then-record Test score of 375 against England. Lara, batting in the County Championship for Warwickshire against Scott's Durham, had reached 18 at Edgbaston when he chased a Simon Brown away-swinger. Scott later described it as 'a very healthy edge but a very straightforward catch, regulation . . . a catch I'd taken a million times before.' The next thing he knew, the ball was on the floor. He reportedly told a fielder: 'Oh dear, he'll probably go on and get a hundred.'

If only. Lara went on to post 501 not out, the highest score ever recorded in first-class cricket and the only time a player has hit a quintuple century. A jaw-dropping 174 of these were scored before lunch on the final day as the match headed for its inevitable draw. No-one in the ground had a better view of Lara's brilliance than the unfortunate Chris Scott.

WEST INDIES, 1998

Four years later, I was back in the West Indies for the 1998 series. Of all England's foreign tours the Caribbean has to be favourite in terms of the social vibes, the people, their love of cricket, the beaches, the rum punches and, generally speaking, the food, although I do recall that we once ate mountain chicken in a Guyana restaurant, which we later discovered was a massive great f***ing frog. But on the whole I thought it was a wonderful place to tour. The only downside was that you had to face perhaps the best fast-bowling unit ever on some of the world's fastest pitches. Fast is one thing and the 1st Test wicket at Sabina Park, Kingston, Jamaica, was certainly that. It was also bloody dangerous.

The game was due to start on 29 January. We'd gone to the ground a couple of days beforehand for some net practice and found two guys sitting on a roller out in the middle, smoking something fairly pungent. I wandered across to ask what they thought of the pitch, might it take a bit of spin, the usual stuff, and then noticed Alec Stewart, Athers and a few of the other batters studying the surface in unusually silent contemplation. The usual bravado was definitely missing. One of the main reasons for this, I gathered, was that the ground staff had banged nails into either end and stretched a piece of string between these to check the levels and height of the cut. Troublingly though, when you got down on hands and knees and looked along the string, some parts of the wicket were above it while others were below. It looked wavy, like corrugated iron. I didn't say anything because I didn't want to put the willies up our batters but every so often one of our guys would get up off all fours, looking pale-faced, and whisper something that didn't seem funny to a team-mate who would then also get down on all fours.

The upshot was that we suspected the pitch would be fruity. But no-one predicted the absolute chaos which ensued when the match started. Once our physio Wayne Morton had tended to the first batting injury he didn't bother going back into the pavilion. He just sat at the boundary gate waiting for the next one and must have been out there 12 times before it became clear the game couldn't continue. Poor old Mark Butcher got brought in on the morning of the match because Jack Russell wasn't fit and Alec had to keep wicket. Butch got a ball that flew off a length, hit his bat handle and left him caught for a duck. I, meanwhile, was watching all this transfixed and petrified, and I wasn't the only one.

Looking back, it was funny because I was the one bloke who always had all the batting protection known to man in his kit bag – chest pad, arm guard, inside thigh pad – and as wickets started to fall players were shuffling over to me saying: 'Tuffers, I couldn't just borrow . . .' to which my reply was: 'Bastard. You always told me I was a chicken for having a chest pad so, no.' However, I did end up handing out all my protection because, with Curtly and Courtney's firepower and balls whistling past your ears, that pitch was deadly. There was a big sigh of relief from me when the match was abandoned because I could have been maimed.

Every cloud has a silver lining, though. It was decided something had to be done for all the supporters who'd spent serious amounts of money flying out for a five-day Test to see precisely 10.1 overs for their trouble. So for every one of those five nights a party was thrown at the British High Commission in Port of Spain, Trinidad, by way of an apology. As players, we were told a bus would collect us, we'd head down, eat vast amounts of free food, have a drink with the fans and generally attempt to entertain and appease them. It was brilliant. I was first on that bus every evening.

Perhaps that set the scene for the tour because I embraced West Indies hospitality and after-match refreshment with alacrity. Specifically, on the eve of the 3rd Test in Port of Spain, with the result that I overslept and missed the team bus on the morning play was due to get underway. It was not the proudest moment of my international career. I hurled every single toy I could find out of the pram and then sat simmering in the back of a taxi, the whole way to the ground. It was a red-hot day, not a breath of wind, and I was obviously cross with myself for having a rum punch too many the night before. But of course it wasn't my fault, because it's never your fault, is it?

On arrival I stumbled, glassy-eyed, into the tiny dressing room at Trinidad where my closest tour mates Mark Ramprakash, Graham Thorpe and Nasser Hussain were just walking out for the warm-up. I tripped over some kit bags, scattered a load of bats and started screaming that they weren't my fecking mates apparently, because otherwise they would have woken me up – just a knock or a phone call would have done – and what bastards they were. But it didn't end there because I then got changed, sprinted out of the pavilion, tripped over some steps and started chasing them around the outfield, where they were jogging with the rest of the team, shouting, 'Call yourselves fecking mates?' Eventually, Ramps, who actually didn't play in that game, said: 'Look, Tuffers, we're not your nursemaids. These boys are going to be facing Curtly and Courtney in a minute. We can't be worrying about you.' Which was fair enough and the only riposte I could think of was a somewhat weak and whiny: 'But you're supposed to wake me up.'

SOUTH AFRICA, 1999

The following year, I was again on England duty overseas – this time in the Test squad to face South Africa. It was a memorable tour for several wrong reasons, not least because it included the infamous Hansie Cronje declaration in the final match which, we later discovered, was done to order for a betting syndicate. But there were some lighter moments and one of my favourites came during the 2nd Test at Port Elizabeth, six months after the end of the World Cup tournament which had been staged in England.

South Africa had looked certain to make the final but in the semis their star fast bowler Allan Donald dropped his bat when called for what would have been the winning run by his batting partner Lance 'Zulu' Klusener. Donald was run out with two balls to spare, the match was tied and that sent opponents Australia through to the final against Pakistan. Make no mistake, the Proteas would have been strongly fancied to beat Pakistan but it was the grateful Aussies who instead blew them away to win the cup. So for Allan the memory of that dropped bat was painfully fresh when it came to playing us. And our Barmy Army travelling support certainly didn't forget.

We always felt like we were paddling against the tide on this tour. We were working hard and fighting for every game, yet still we were getting battered. However, that didn't stop the Army enjoying themselves. They had arrived in South Africa when the exchange rate was something like 20 rand to the pound so they were getting a good bang for their buck at the venue bars. Their songs got longer and better, and it felt like the worse our results the better they performed. They enlivened a long day in the field, provided plenty of light relief to cheer us up and when they hit on the idea of teasing Allan – one of the Proteas' most feared attacking threats – with their version of 'Da Doo Ron Ron' by the Crystals, it was a comic masterstroke.

> *My name is Allan Donald and I should have run;*
> *Run, run, Allan-run, run, run, run, run;*
> *Zulu called a single but I stood still;*
> *Run, run, Allan-run, run, run, run, run*
> *Ooh! I had a panic attack*
> *Ooh! And then I dropped my bat,*
> *Ooh! We could have won the cup if*
> *I'd run run, run Allan, run, run, run*

NICE LINE
The Barmy Army

As Aggers has pointed out, the origins of the Barmy Army arguably date to England's 1990–1 tour of Australia when England fans were first grouped together in a corner of the WACA in Perth. They embraced the name given to them by the Australian press, whose logic was that supporters who travel halfway around the world to watch their team continually get beaten must be barmy. By the 1994–5 Ashes tour, the Army had adopted an altogether more formal set-up with three supporters – Paul Burnham, David Peacock and Gareth Evans – credited with transforming it from a dissolute group of backpackers into a world-renowned international supporters club. It is now a limited company and arranges tickets and tour packages for all England's overseas series.

It can't have affected Allan that much because he took three wickets in our first innings. But he perhaps wasn't at his absolute best because, although we needed 302 in our second, Nasser Hussain's stubborn 70 meant we somehow escaped with a draw despite being six down. I actually did OK in that game, taking four wickets. But if I felt a surge of confidence, the next Test at Durban, which began on Boxing Day, soon snuffed it out.

By the third day of that match, we were on the cusp of a famous victory. Having amassed 366 in our first innings we ran through the South African batting order to dismiss them for a paltry 156. Nasser Hussain duly enforced the follow-on and it just needed a repeat performance for us to finish early and indulge in some proper festive celebrations with our families. As principal bowler on a wearing wicket, I was expected to bear the brunt of the bowling and make it all happen. It was my domain because the seamers can't be huffing and puffing all the time through long, hot sessions. This was where I really should have earned my corn.

It all seemed to be going swimmingly when I trapped the dangerous Gary Kirsten plumb lbw when he was on 33. But then the umpire signalled 'no-ball' and Gary cracked on for another 12 desperate hours – desperate for me, not him – in which he scored 275 off 642 balls to ensure the match was drawn. I sweated through 45 overs in that second innings without a thing to show for it and walked off feeling like the Grinch who stole Christmas. I couldn't come out of my hotel room because I thought all the kids would be pointing at me as the horrible guy who kept their dad away.

For the most part, Christmas on tour with England is a bit understated. You're usually about to start a match, you're focused on that; you might stop the bus en route to somewhere and have a few drinks but it's never the same experience you get at home. For one thing, several of the Test-playing nations don't really celebrate Christmas so if you're in those countries it can feel a bit awkward and inappropriate. Having said that, an early finish to that 3rd Test would certainly have been a memorable Christmas in the England camp, not least because we'd probably have won.

We were blown away in the 4th Test at Cape Town with Donald back to his best. Which meant South Africa were 2–0 up and had secured a series win going into the final match at Centurion. That game is now seen as the moment international cricket finally woke up to the risk of betting scams and fixed results. We'd lost so much time to rain that it seemed a draw was inevitable until the home captain Hansie Cronje offered Nasser a deal in which both sides would effectively forfeit an innings and South Africa would set a gettable target. Nasser accepted and we chased down 249 with two wickets left. Against their attack, in two sessions, that seemed a good effort, but South Africa had won the series anyway so Cronje's generous offer didn't look particularly strange. When we later discovered he'd taken a bung we were as shocked as anyone.

The mood in the England dressing room was that Hansie had made a fantastic gesture. There were about 5000 travelling supporters who had been out there skulking under umbrellas for three days without seeing any cricket. Some had come over just for that one Test match and here was a chance for everyone to at least see a competitive match rather than sit and watch an uneventful game limp into a dull draw with a festival of forward-defensive strokes. Declarations like the one offered by Cronje had never really been done before in Test cricket, perhaps because it was considered too sacred a vehicle for a contrived result. But it was not unheard of in county games.

Looking back on my England touring career, I always felt I had to try twice as hard as anyone else to get the same praise and plaudits. And in a way that was quite good for me because it *did* make me try harder. Whether the stereotype was right or not, I don't know. Nasser, in his memoir, said I was a great tourist to have along but if you were to ask Goochie he'd say I was a nightmare. There's certainly now a recognition that 16 players are likely to need different preparation techniques – what's the point in everyone going off for a 16-mile run when the batters perhaps don't need that as much as the bowlers? I was accused of having a bad attitude to weights and gym work but there was no point in me building up muscles in the gym because I never needed muscle to bowl a cricket ball and I never lacked fitness. Fitness and strength are important to help avoid injuries but there is now a lot more one-to-one skills-based preparation. You tailor it and don't place it above coaching and technical work.

I was selected more often for overseas tours than I was for home Tests and that annoyed me because I took a lot of wickets for Middlesex on English pitches. But I guess the counties have always wanted greener tracks to assist swing and seam bowlers whereas the hotter, drier wickets abroad are seen as more suited to spin. On tour, spinners were also regarded as useful workhorses who could perform a holding role to restrict any batter who got well set. I certainly did do that job but I think my record showed I offered a bit more too.

TOP LIST

Best batters you've bowled to or watched

AGGERS Viv Richards. I don't think I've seen another batsman who owned the batting crease like Viv did.

TUFFERS The name Brian Charles Lara is lasered into my memory. In 1994 I had the pleasure of bowling at him for two-and-a-half desperate days in Antigua as he cruised in chanceless manner to his then world record score of 375. At first, England players thought he was lucky because his shots always seemed to just miss fielders. As time went on, we realised that he *meant* to just miss them. He could have hit a teacup on the boundary if he'd wanted. One of the true greats.

ISA I love watching Joe Root play spin but the best performance I ever saw was in 2001 when V. V. S. Laxman built that incredible 370-odd fifth-wicket partnership with Rahul Dravid in Kolkata. It still haunts Australia to this day because they had forced India to follow on. Shane Warne was bowling around the wicket into the rough and Laxman would hit him over midwicket. But then an identical delivery would be swatted through extra cover. It was a ridiculous show of ability against high-class spin, a total masterclass. In the second innings, Laxman hit 281, Dravid 180 and India won by 171 runs. As for the best against fast bowling, I can't see beyond Sachin Tendulkar. I'll never forget him smashing Brett Lee back over Brett's head.

EBONY Against the quicks it would be Brian Lara. When he got
in the zone his backswing got higher and higher, and he would
demolish even the very quickest. He could pull in front of square
when everyone else pulled behind. He had so much time it was
ridiculous. Against spin, it must be Sachin Tendulkar. He tore up all
the rules I'd learned – don't play against the spin, go forward to this
length, back to that length. Sachin wrote his own set of rules and the
more a ball turned, the easier he managed it.

CARLOS The former Australian opener Matthew Hayden would
pummel fast bowling and fight fire with fire. But right up there with
him would be Shiv Chanderpaul, who could dead-bat immaculately
if necessary and then switch to attack in a heartbeat.

ALISON The best batting performance I personally witnessed was
Kevin Pietersen's counterattack on Brett Lee at the Oval in the final
2005 Ashes Test – a passage of play that turned the Ashes in
England's favour. You just thought: 'Wow.'

AATIF India's Vinod Kambli during a club game when I was very
young. He scored 160 not out and it was all pretty brutal. But I went
for only eight runs off my two overs, which I claimed as a huge win.

CHAPTER 8

SPECIAL SUMMERS – THE AUSSIES IN ENGLAND

In which the team recalls the joys of some
Ashes summers on English soil – and that
famous World Cup win at Lord's.

THE ASHES, 1993

TUFFERS

Of all the great players on both sides who have contested an Ashes series, the one that stands out for me is Shane Warne. I was playing in the 1st Ashes Test at Old Trafford in June 1993 when he got Gatting out with his 'ball of the century', a dagger to the heart of the England dressing room. I'd bowled well that day, spun a few, picked up the wickets of Mark Waugh and Ian Healy, and we were pretty happy to restrict them to 289. So we were quietly congratulating ourselves as we sat in the pavilion to watch Shane bowl for the first time in England. There was a lot of 'who is this kid with the blond highlights and the earring' and 'he seems a bit flash and fancy'. So we're all gathered around the telly to have a look at him, casually drinking our cuppas, and he goes and bowls his first ball in Test cricket in England which turns 2½ feet and takes Mike Gatting's off stump. People say that, as a spinner, if you can spin it the width of a bat you're doing well. On this occasion, Shane spun it the width of a Gatt, and that was some width!

The room fell absolutely silent, there was a bit of throat clearing and shuffling of feet, and then Robin Smith broke the tension by asking me: 'Tuffers, what *have* you been doing all these years?' In the press, we started reading these names Shane had for his deliveries – a slider, a zooter. I mean, what the fecking hell was a zooter?

You talk to the batters now and they'll tell you he had this ability to suffocate scoring and then suddenly explode into a four- or five-for. He was a showman and he emptied the bars whenever he bowled.

AGGERS

My *TMS* commentary for that first Warne delivery went: 'Shane Warne, off only two or three paces and Gatting is taken on the pads . . . he's bowled! Well, Gatting is still standing there. He can't believe it but that must have turned a very long way . . . we'll have to wait for a replay to tell you exactly what happened.'

There was so much talk about Shane Warne and his first over was much anticipated. We'd never seen him live before. I was criticised for my commentary but the fact is that he was bowling from the far end, Ian Healy was standing up at the stumps and Mike Gatting was in front of them. I couldn't see what Warne's delivery did off the pitch but Healy was jumping up and down, Gatting was squared up and I realised he'd been bowled. I just couldn't explain *how* he was bowled. It was only when the replay arrived that the incredible spin Warne had imparted on the ball became obvious. People may now say it was a bit of a commentary shambles but, believe me, calling it live was impossible.

THE ASHES, 2001

TUFFERS

England had already lost the Ashes when it came to the final Test of that 2001 summer. I knew it was the end of my international career when, in his press conference before the game, I heard our coach Duncan Fletcher answering questions about my fellow spinner Ashley Giles's injury. He told journalists, words to the effect: 'I've had a look round and Tufnell's the only spinner I can find.' Which roughly translated meant: 'I don't want him but he's all we've got. Everyone else is injured or crap.' It was hardly a ringing endorsement. We lost the toss at the Oval, they batted first, Langer got 102, the Waugh brothers 277 between them and the Aussies finally declared on 641 for 4. Mark Ramprakash hit a brilliant 133 in the first innings but we folded in the second to give them a 4–1 series victory and the continuation of a winning streak which dated back to 1989. Warne got 11 wickets in the match at an average of 20.8 whereas I finished with figures of 1–174. But even if I'd got a ten-for it wouldn't have made any difference. Afterwards, I picked up my kit and thought: 'That's me done.'

We lost the game by an innings and 25 runs but, unusually in an England–Australia game, one of my team-mates won the sledging war with arguably the best line ever on English soil. Step forward Jimmy Ormond, a medium-fast bowler who was making his international debut after performing consistently well for Leicestershire over several seasons. Jimmy was 6ft 3in, a big unit, and not one for taking a step back. He must have known he was going to get a verbal roasting from the Aussies and I suspect he'd considered possible ripostes. A little basic research served him well.

The Waughs, who are twin brothers, had both done well in that game and both were obviously world-class all-rounders. But the record showed Steve's stats were better and by the time they later retired from Test cricket, it was Steve who came out on top with 10,927 runs and 92 Test wickets against Mark's 8029 and 59. So when Jimmy Ormond walked out to bat he must have been quietly hoping Mark would start the sledge fest. He was not disappointed: 'Look who it is. Mate, what are you doing out here? There's no way you're good enough to play for England.' Ormond shrugged. 'Maybe not,' he replied, 'but at least I'm the best player in my family.' *Touché*.

Steve Waugh used to call sledging 'mental deterioration' and it was a dark art the Aussies had long mastered. They had the attitude that there were eleven of them on the field, and only two of us batting, so if they worked together they could get us out of our comfort zone. Fast bowler Merv Hughes was among the best exponents – particularly with Graeme Hick at the crease – and I was also a popular target. Once at the Gabba, with Shane Warne about to bowl, one of the Aussie slips shouted: 'Hey, Tuffers, can I borrow your brain? I'm building an idiot.' It worked too because I looked round. But at least it was clean.

For me, sledging can be counterproductive. I was quite an aggressive spin bowler, long run-up, long follow-through, and as I started in cricket as a fast bowler I had that in-your-face approach towards batters. But if you're not careful you fire up certain players. Why on earth would you want to make Viv Richards cross? There's an argument that the fielding side should avoid speaking to batters, especially if they are known to like a chat, to make them feel isolated. But that's not fool-proof either. It certainly didn't end well when we tried it on Brian Lara in Antigua because he went on to score his world-record 375-run innings.

NICE LINE
Aussie sledging classics

An old favourite of Australian pace legend Dennis Lillee was to tell an opponent he understood why he was playing so badly: 'It's because you've got some shit on the end of your bat.' The hapless victim would raise his bat to check the toe-end, at which point Dennis would sneer: 'Wrong end, mate.' His countryman Merv Hughes was a similarly formidable sledger who, on beating South African-born England batter Robin Smith's outside edge, informed him: 'You can't f***ing bat.' Smith, equally feisty, stayed quiet but smashed Hughes's next ball to the boundary. 'Hey, Merv,' he chirped cheerily, 'don't we make a fine pair? I can't f***ing bat and you can't f***ing bowl.'

Another South African fond of a stumps-side chat was Daryll Cullinan, a player who ended his career with a Test average of more than 44 but who was seen as something of a rabbit against Shane Warne. On one occasion, Cullinan returned from a long injury lay-off to face the Aussie spinner. 'I've been waiting two years for the opportunity to humiliate you in front of your own crowd,' Warne told him. Cullinan's response was perfectly timed: 'Looks like you spent it eating.'

THE ASHES, 2005

AGGERS

This was one of the great contests of recent years because it involved brilliant cricket and results that could have gone either way. Australia were narrow favourites. They'd won the Ashes every year since 1989 and in those 16 barren years England had lost every Ashes series, apart from 1997, by more than one Test match. The tourists were also the top-rated Test side and their talisman Glenn McGrath had even suggested a 5–0 win for the tourists was a serious possibility. And yet England under Michael Vaughan were on a good run. They'd won 14 and drawn 3 of their previous 18 Test matches and were ranked No. 2 in the world.

The 1st Test at Lord's seemed to support McGrath's analysis. Australia won easily by 239 runs – thanks largely to his nine wickets – and the only real positives for England lay in the performances of debutant Kevin Pietersen, who scored 57 and 64 not out, and paceman Steve Harmison, who finished with 8–97. All of us in the press box were demanding changes to the team but Michael insisted it should stay the same. That was a big call and one of the defining moments which helped England retain the Ashes.

Another was that English crowds were more vociferous in their support, and more hostile towards the visitors, than had been the case for many a year. I first noticed this in the T20 game at

Southampton when Jason Gillespie and Michael Kasprowicz got slogged and the crowd really started to get at them. Then Australia lost a one-day game against Bangladesh in Cardiff and, once again, the crowd gave them an unusually hard time. It marked a shift in the way English crowds support their team and it continued very obviously at both Old Trafford and Trent Bridge. On the field, it felt as though the Australians had lost the fear factor that so often assisted their game. I wonder if this was because so many of their key players had signed for county clubs – the likes of Shane Warne, Glenn McGrath – and English players had seen them in the showers and chatted to them after games and realised that, for all the snarling out in the middle, they were actually just normal, nice blokes. The mystique had gone.

The 2nd Test at Edgbaston ranks among the greatest I've ever seen. Things started going well from an English perspective before a ball was even bowled when Glenn McGrath trod on a stray cricket ball while playing rugby in the warm-up. He was ruled out of the game with torn ankle ligaments, leaving England to face the far lesser threat of Kasprowicz. Bafflingly, Ricky Ponting then stuck England into bat, whereupon Marcus Trescothick embarked on a ruthless demolition of Brett Lee in a 112-run partnership with Andrew Strauss. England scored at four an over to finish the day on 407 – the first team ever to hit 400 runs on the first day of a Test match against Australia – and you did wonder whether this was a momentum shift. The match ebbed and flowed until, on the fourth day, Ponting's side was left needing 107 to win with just two wickets left. Mopping up the tail seemed a formality for the England bowlers but a magnificent rearguard action saw first Warne and Lee add 45 for the ninth wicket and then Kasprowicz and Lee take the Aussies to within three runs of a famous victory. But then Kasprowicz fended a short, fast ball from Harmison off his glove and was given out caught behind, an error by umpire Billy Bowden as the glove was not in contact with the bat. Nonetheless England – who had been one shot away from going 2–0 down in the series – were declared the winners. A despondent Brett Lee sank to his haunches and that provided one of the most poignant images of the entire series as Freddie Flintoff, who had taken seven wickets in the match, bent over to console him. For all the raw aggression on the field, it was a heart-warming gesture which summed up the mutual respect between the teams.

That brought us to Old Trafford and another desperately tight denouement. As the final day got underway, Australia were 24 for 0, still needing 399 to win. Had they managed this it would have been a record fourth innings total to win a Test match and it speaks volumes for their collective character that they made it look possible. But when Clarke and Gillespie both succumbed in quick succession, and Ponting's defiant seven hours at the crease ended with him on 156, the visitors only focus was survival. Lee and McGrath's last-wicket stand over the final four overs delivered that and the Australian dressing room erupted in joy. I was commentating at the time and I made the point that it was highly unusual to see Australia massively celebrating a draw. I know it was noted by the England players too and I suspect this was the moment they realised they had the firepower to win back the Ashes.

It certainly seemed as though Ricky Ponting was rattled. Especially when, on the third day of the 4th Test, he was run out through a superb pick-up-and-throw by England's substitute fielder Gary Pratt. It came just as the hosts were losing the initiative despite posting a first innings total of 477 thanks to a Flintoff century and 85 from Geraint Jones. Simon Jones's 5–44 had allowed Vaughan to enforce the follow-on – the first time any Australian side had suffered such ignominy in 17 years – but the Aussies then fought back in the evening session and Jones had to leave the field with an ankle injury. With Ponting easing towards his half-century he was called for a single only to see new boy Pratt hurl a direct hit on to the stumps from extra cover.

It was a pivotal moment and the Aussie skipper knew it. As he walked back to the pavilion his ice-cool image suddenly shattered and he turned on England's coach Duncan Fletcher, who was understandably smiling down from the pavilion at this turn of events. It was the kind of invective an Aussie sheep shearer searching fruitlessly for a cold beer in the Outback might have unleashed. The background was that Ponting had got it into his head that England were overusing Pratt as their sub. He felt this was cheating because it allowed bowlers to go off for a rest while ensuring England could deploy one of the best outfielders in the world. Yet England had broken no rules and Pratt was certainly entitled to be on the field given Jones's injury.

The following day England went on to score the 129 needed for victory, although they had to rely on their Nos 8 and 9, Ashley Giles and Matthew Hoggard, to see them home. But they were still some way from reclaiming The Ashes. A win in the final Test would have allowed Australia to retain the urn and while the tourists had Glenn McGrath back in action – he'd missed Trent Bridge with an elbow injury – Simon Jones had not recovered in time. To some raised eyebrows in the press box, England picked all-rounder Paul Collingwood ahead of their inexperienced but dangerous fast bowler, James Anderson, to play at the Oval.

As the fifth day got underway, the entire series rested on the proverbial knife edge. England started well and rode their luck thanks to a couple of dropped catches but then McGrath and Warne took two wickets apiece before lunch to leave Vaughan's side on 133 for 5 and a lead of just 139. Any middle-order collapse would have given Australia the chance to snatch victory and few doubted they would take it. England sides of the past might have gone into their shell and played for time but now things were different. Far from batting defensively, Kevin Pietersen launched a devastating counterattack with some of the most incredible shots I've ever seen. Brett Lee bowled a really hostile spell but Pietersen just took him on – hooking him for sixes and fours and totally dominating the Aussie attack. He finished on 158, ably supported by Giles and Collingwood, and with the light fading it became clear Australia would never have enough time to score the 342 they needed to win. They accepted a bad-light offer from the umpires and at 18:17 the bails were removed and the party began.

TUFFERS

The first thing to say is: what a wonderful summer to be a *TMS* summariser. I felt like a kid of 16 again turning up, sitting in the stand watching it all unfold and having the best seat in the house. At the Oval, I was singing 'Ashes Coming Home' to the tune of 'Three Lions' live on air. I finally realised what I was doing and had to apologise to everyone. We're not supposed to be quite so biased. It wasn't a great apology because I unconvincingly claimed the song had 'just slipped out'.

England had been on a good run, they had some great players, and they felt and looked like a team. But there was something more to it than that and a lot of the credit has to go to Michael Vaughan both tactically on the field and in his man management off it. At Lord's, on the morning of the 1st Test, he later told me how MCC members in the Long Room were standing, clapping, roaring and cheering as England took the field. I mean, hold on, this is the Long Room. You're usually lucky to get a smattering of polite applause. But there was a feeling in the country that this England team could do it, that something was afoot, and I think we managed to relay that in our commentary. Even though England lost the match at Lord's, they fully looked the part and their supporters knew it. By the time we got to the final day of the 3rd Test at Old Trafford, there were more than 10,000 outside the ground just wanting to be there.

The great privilege of working for *TMS* is that you have fantastic vantage points and we picked up on that Trent Bridge tirade from Ricky straight away. We could clearly see he'd lost the famous

Ponting inscrutability; the whole cool, calm, collected, controlled approach to captaincy had gone up in smoke. He was scowling and swearing loudly in the direction of the England dressing room and it was as though the scales fell from our eyes, the moment we realised the Aussies were under serious pressure and things weren't going to plan for them. It's remarkable how you sense these momentum shifts in the *TMS* box. It's almost a sixth sense. You get a feeling, perhaps founded on your own playing career, that someone or some team is on a roll and it's time to stop talking about the cake and devour the cricket instead.

You can't deny that a few things went England's way in the series. For instance, Glenn McGrath treading on a ball at Edgbaston and getting ruled out of that game. How big was that? Then minutes later Ponting, without his star bowler, winning the toss and opting to bowl. To bowl? On a perfect batting track with the sun shining? We were looking at each other totally mystified. We all felt Ponting had handed the initiative to England and, certainly on that first day, we were bang on. To smash the Aussies for more than 400 runs before the close was a huge statement of intent and one they weren't used to. That's what *they* did to opponents. You also have to say, however, that it was a measure of the Australian team that they fought back and took the match to what was at the time the most exciting finish in modern Ashes history.

ALISON

I was a boundary commentator for 5 Live at the Oval Test so I had a great view of Kevin Pietersen's assault on Brett Lee's bowling from ground level, sitting on the grass just beyond the rope, leaning my back against the advertising hoarding. I particularly remember the banter from the crowd towards the end of that match when play had been stopped for bad light. The Aussie fans were putting on sunglasses, pretending it was bright sunshine and urging the umpires to get the teams back out, while England fans were putting up umbrellas to suggest the rain was so bad the game should go to its inevitable draw.

AGGERS

When England finally won the Ashes after that drawn 5th Test, I
headed into their dressing room to interview the players. There
wasn't a single one in there because they were all in the Australian
dressing room. And that summed up the series. It was hard fought,
there were a few tantrums, harsh words were said, but in the
moment it was over they were all just cricketers having a beer
together after the game. The following day, I was the only journalist
allowed to join the England team on their open-top bus tour around
London, which was an extraordinary spectacle in itself. I was
broadcasting a live feed from my microphone to a helicopter
tracking the bus and so we had to maintain a straight line of sight
between the two of us. Every now and then the signal would
inevitably break up but as soon as the helicopter came back into
view I knew I was good to get some exclusive player reaction, given
that I was the only broadcaster on the bus.

The ECB press officer said I could interview anyone I liked except
Andrew Flintoff. Really? Anyone but the man of the series then? All
the wives and girlfriends were on board so when I saw Freddie
sitting with his wife Rachael up at the front, holding his young
daughter, I reasoned that if I addressed questions to Rachael the
inevitable would happen and Freddie would pitch in too. Which is
precisely what did happen. Within 30 seconds this huge moon face
hove into view and a completely smashed Andrew held forth live.
The BBC kept playing it all day and I remember wondering, as
I drove home that evening, whether that was entirely wise.

Interviewing a smashed Freddie live was one thing but repeating it all day? It quickly sparked a debate on whether players should be celebrating by over-indulgence in alcohol.

My clearest memory though was the bus turning into Trafalgar Square. The players genuinely didn't think anyone would bother turning up but every last inch of it was jampacked, red, white and blue everywhere, an incredible atmosphere and unbelievable noise. They were still taking it in when they arrived in Downing Street to meet Prime Minister Tony Blair. We'd been quite a long time on the bus and of course legend has it that Freddie excused himself briefly to 'water the garden'. All I can say to that is that I couldn't possibly comment as I wasn't invited into Downing Street. It was an amazing day but the whole open-top bus thing really niggled the Australians and was all grist to their mill when they whitewashed England 5–0 in the following Ashes series 18 months later.

THE ASHES, 2015

AGGERS

It's always a great achievement to win the Ashes, yet looking back over the early noughties, this one somehow always goes under the radar. It was a big challenge for Alastair Cook because a lot was going on in the background. He'd been pilloried over his supposed role in ending Kevin Pietersen's England career, his side had been whitewashed 5–0 during the previous 2013–14 Ashes in Australia and sections of the media were persistently questioning his position as captain. But Alastair is one of the most stubborn people I've ever met. He's a very good friend of mine and he'll chuckle when he reads that but it's true. The fact is that if you're an opening bat and captain of your country, you jolly well *have* to be stubborn, especially if you're doing what he did for so long. You have to shut out everything, make your own decisions, be your own man. But he also had the sense to take advice from a former Ashes-winning England captain in Michael Vaughan and that was pivotal in his team's 3–2 series win.

There was a lot of talk about the way the pitches were prepared; they were very slow, they turned, the selectors obviously had England's proven Ashes winner Graeme Swann in mind and, of course, these things were a factor which frustrated the Australians. But actually the player who definitively won that series was Stuart

Broad who, in one of the most extraordinary fast-bowling spells I've ever witnessed, destroyed the cream of Australian batting in under two hours at Trent Bridge. All the pre-series talk had focused on Jimmy Anderson but Jimmy wasn't fit for that game so Stuart had to stand up and lead the attack. And actually, whenever that's happened, he's always done it rather well. Bowling the Aussies out before lunch for 60 was an incredible feat, there was no way back for them and it put England 3–1 up with one to play.

TUFFERS

Sometimes the match-winning moments in a Test are immediately obvious. You see the first three balls swinging around and within the *TMS* team you're asking each other: 'What d'you reckon? Over by tea on the third day?' That was certainly how it felt on the first morning of that 2015 Trent Bridge Test when Stuart Broad returned figures of 9.3–5–15–8 to dismiss Australia for the shortest first innings in Test history – just 111 balls. On his home ground, with the crowd behind him and the ball moving, you could tell from the moment he had opener Chris Rogers caught at slip third ball that he was on fire. He knew it, the Aussies knew it and if you're the batter you do not want to be facing Stuart in that mood. As a player you know when someone is on it, that he's changing the game, that a win is on – and it's the same in the commentary box.

NICE LINE

Broadside at the Bridge

Trent Bridge, the first day of the 2015 4th Ashes Test, England 2–1 up in the series but missing their inspirational fast bowler Jimmy Anderson. The attack was to be led by Stuart Broad – no mean performer himself – who was on the cusp of claiming his 300th Test wicket. That 300th scalp was secured with his third ball although in the context of what happened next it hardly mattered. Broad went on to bowl the greatest nine-over spell ever seen in the modern game on English soil.

His figures – 9.3–5–15–8 – are jaw-dropping in themselves. But the manner in which they were achieved almost defies description. Broad, with a little support from Mark Wood and Steven Finn, inflicted on Australia – Australia – the shortest first innings ever recorded in a Test match. It lasted a mere 111 balls, beating the 113 balls England took to see off the Aussies at Lord's in 1896, and the first four batters managed only 12 balls between them as the tourists collapsed to 60 all out. It was only the fourth time ever that a team had been bowled out before lunch on the first day. *TMS*'s Henry Blofeld noted that 'no script writers – even Sam Mendes in all those James Bond films – could have written this'. Australian commentators were rather less kind. *TMS*'s Jim Maxwell called it 'one of the most embarrassing batting performances in Test history', while the *Sydney Morning Herald*'s sports editor didn't waste words: 'It's Pomicide', read the headline. England went on to win the match by an innings and 78 runs and ultimately took the series 3–2.

ENGLAND V. NEW ZEALAND, 2019 WORLD CUP

AGGERS

This has been called the match of the decade and in the one-day arena you can't argue with that. It was raw, pure sporting theatre, the game that just kept on giving, and it's hard to see what else you could have thrown into the mix to keep Lord's agog. There was New Zealand's Trent Boult's match-winning catch – until he stepped on the boundary rope. There was Ben Stokes's deflection of an incoming throw which raced for six overthrows when the umpires should have signalled five. There was the loss of England's last two wickets when they needed just three off two balls, which left the game proper tied. Then that final ball of the Super Over, which saw Martin Guptill diving for his crease to complete a winning run, only to be run out by a superb Jason Roy throw. The Super Over was therefore also tied but both teams knew what that meant. The rules stated that, if all else failed, a boundary countback would decide the champions and the countback was 26–17 in England's favour.

In those last incredible moments my *TMS* commentary ran: *It's come to this. Here's the last ball of the World Cup final, Archer bowls it. It's clipped away into the legside, they're going to come back for the second, the throw comes in to the wicketkeeper's end . . . He's run out . . . is he? England think he's run out. England are convinced he's been run out . . .*

I took some criticism for that commentary because people pointed out that Guptill finished a good 2 metres short and it should have been immediately obvious he was out. But this is the lot of the cricket commentator. It's dead easy to make such calls when you're watching from a side-on camera in slow motion. There was no way on earth we could have ruled definitively on that in real time from our commentary position at Lord's. No chance. You're looking at the ball coming in, Jos Buttler taking the ball, Guptill running and diving away from me at full pelt, the stumps broken – it was just impossible. It didn't do me any favours because when Ben Stokes won BBC Sports Personality of the Year later that year, my commentary was played against a slow-motion side-on replay, which seemed rather harsh. If you make a mistake you make a mistake but, at times, it's a bit hard to take. This one rankled a bit.

TUFFERS

Michael Vaughan and I were due to summarise for the last half-hour of the game but our slots then got extended for the Super Overs. It was just as well that Aggers was anchoring everything because Michael and I got so wrapped up in it. There was Jon, the ultimate professional, rising above the madness, describing the bowler's run-up, the batter's shot, the fielder's return, whereas I'd turned into a fully paid-up fan. My contribution was to scream over Aggers: 'RUN, RUN' or 'OH NO, WHAT'S HE DOING?' or 'YOU'LL NEVER SEE ANOTHER GAME OF CRICKET LIKE THIS.' That last observation turned out to be wrong because a month later at Headingley Ben Stokes hit that incredible 135 not out to win the 3rd Ashes Test by one wicket.

When it came to the Super Over, Aggers was brilliantly calm whereas I was virtually shouting out my comments. As a summariser you can get away with it because you don't have to do the essential ball-by-ball lines – you're free to talk about great shots and great deliveries and you get wrapped up in it all and start loving the moment. As for that final Super Over, I think only Aggers knew the rules, and thank God he did. He was the only man you'd want at the mic when that last ball was struck to Jason Roy. To be able to explain what was happening in a match-winning moment, to bring it to life, talking at speed and with clarity, a combination of excitement and precision – that's a very special skill which I certainly don't have. Then the whole box, apart from our Kiwi summariser Jeremy Coney who was understandably despondent, just leapt up – commentators, technicians, electricians, the lot of us – because of course we all wanted England to win. I don't think I've ever experienced sensory overload like it.

We did also pay tribute to New Zealand for their role in an astonishing game. They were a thoroughly class act in defeat, which surprised nobody because they are one of the most gracious and sporting teams you'll find in any sport, not just cricket. Whereas I would have been going absolutely mental, probably crying, believing I'd been robbed, they lined up, shook hands, applauded England and behaved immaculately. To a large extent that's the influence of their captain Kane Williamson, a gentleman of the game. And the truth is, aside from that tournament boundary-countback rule, there was nothing in the Laws of Cricket to separate two magnificent teams.

THE ASHES, 2019

AGGERS

This was a series defined by one glorious, surreal, summer afternoon in Leeds. It almost feels like the other four games in the series have since been airbrushed out and, for most England fans, they probably have been. But you have to mention some outstanding performances. Right at the top was former Australian captain Steve Smith, imperious in every match apart from Headingley, which he missed as a precaution following a concussion scare. He became the first batsman in Test history to register ten successive scores of 50 or more against a single opponent. There were also some great bowling performances – on England's side two six-fors from Jofra Archer and consistent wicket-taking by Stuart Broad; on Australia's Hazlewood, Cummins and Lyon, who all recorded good hauls. But history can be a fickle mistress and in this series she cares only about the hot afternoon of Sunday 25 August, the fourth day of the Headingley Test, England's last two men at the crease, a distant target and a rampant Australian attack. We'd reached this point after Australia were bowled out for a disappointing 179 in their first innings, England responded with a truly parlous 67, the Aussies hit a further 246 and England, now set 359 to win, needing to keep the series alive by scoring 113 more than either side had managed in the three innings to date. In the low-scoring context of the game, on a wearing pitch, this was off-the-scale unlikely.

For a while, Root, Denly and Bairstow had given England's supporters some fragile, Panglossian hope. But when Buttler and Woakes were both out for a single apiece, Jofra Archer fell for 15 and Stuart Broad was dispatched second ball for a duck, a reality check kicked in. England's tail-ender Jack Leach – who in the first innings appeared to have scarpered across his crease to avoid a Hazlewood rocket which blew away leg stump – would surely not survive. As he strode out to join Ben Stokes, then on 61, England needed 73 runs. There would be no miracle. Until there was.

In fairness to Leach, he had made 92 against Ireland the previous month. But this Australian attack was a different beast. Until the skittling of England's middle order, Stokes had batted cautiously by his standards; now he knew he had to both farm the strike and take every opportunity to score. He first targeted Nathan Lyon, smashing four sixes including one extraordinary switch-hit into the Western Terrace. Then he turned on Hazlewood, belting a four to bring up his century followed by two audacious sixes. The tourists' skipper Tim Paine brought back Cummins, the world's leading fast bowler, who Stokes promptly dispatched for successive fours. And slowly, subtly, the pressure shifted from batsmen to fielders. Two tough catching chances were dropped – chances a less tense Aussie side might have pouched – and suddenly England needed just eight to win. Stokes refused two singles off Lyon, then smashed him over mid-off for six. He reverse-swept the fifth ball to backward point and in that moment it all so nearly went wrong as Leach charged down the wicket for a single and was immediately sent back. He scrambled home only because

Cummins's throw was slightly wayward and Lyon dropped the ball as it arrived.

The final agony for Australia came when Lyon's last ball, full and straight, struck Stokes on the pad as he missed an attempted sweep. It looked a decent lbw shout but umpire Joe Wilson turned it down. If only Paine hadn't used his last, desperate review during the previous over from Cummins it might have been different. But he *had* used it and in the next over Leach, who had been relentlessly polishing his glasses between overs, unnerving England fans, stepped up. After resolutely defending 17 balls he got off the mark with a single and four balls later it was all over as Stokes hammered yet another four to end on 135 not out and win the match. He rightly got all the plaudits. But Leach's defiance was every bit as crucial.

I doubt there will ever be another summer of cricket in England like 2019. You had the greatest finish to a one-day game imaginable and, I would argue, the greatest Test match innings that will ever be played. And all within six weeks of each other. It was absolutely incredible. I feel lucky and honoured to be the person given the responsibility of commenting on them and I felt the whole *TMS* team did a great job – not least Alastair Cook, who was doing his first Test with us at Headingley. The games had everything – fun, tension, sporting tragedy, controversy, brilliance, a hero in Ben Stokes, an unsung hero in Jack Leach and a wonderfully sporting Australian team who, to a man, congratulated Stokes in his moment of triumph. If you ask me to choose between Stokes's innings at Lord's and Headingley then I'm always going to say Headingley, partly because I love Test cricket but also because there was so much depth to what happened.

Any decent international team can go out and win a one-off one-day game. But that Test was unique. We'll never see the like of it again and, yes, I know people will say that 'never' is a big word, but it's true. Quite aside from the magnificence of Stokes, the game was turned from lost to won on fine margins such as Australia running out of reviews, Nathan Lyon missing the run out, Leach surviving for so long against all the odds and – overarching the whole show – the Ashes at stake. I shamelessly say that the Headingley game was what puts Test cricket above all other forms of the game. It is a mark of how much it affected Australia because, although the series ended 2–2, meaning they retained the Ashes, they looked very downcast after losing the final match at the Oval. They knew they should have won the urn outright.

The Hundred tournament in 2021 was good fun and good entertainment but that's true of all cricket. And games like the Lord's World Cup final will always be talked about. But in truth Test matches have got the depth and resonance which one-day cricket can never have. If I was pushed, I reckon I could remember most of the 350-odd Tests I've seen – not always the game itself but perhaps a dinner with friends and colleagues or some bizarre journey to get to a venue. But of the one-day games I've seen, say, in the past year, there are plenty I'd struggle to remember.

After Stokes's Headingley knock we were watching video clips posted on social media of celebrations across the country – strangers gathering around radios on parks and beaches, club cricket matches paused for the final overs – and of course you don't think about this happening while you're commentating for *TMS* because you're focused solely on the moment. Often, I feel I'm almost commentating to myself. To be able to take our listeners to great sporting moments like that, and hopefully do them justice, is a fabulous feeling.

TOP LIST

Best sledging line

AGGERS 'You're much less handsome than you sound on the radio.' Australian taxi driver to me in 2006.

TUFFERS A welcome to the crease from an Aussie slip fielder: 'Tuffers, can I borrow your brain? I'm building an idiot.'

ISA Not a sledging line but a sweet. I've known a player to arrange Love Hearts on the crease for an incoming batter.

CHAPTER 9

COMMENTARY BOX LEGENDS

~~~~~~

In which Aggers recalls some of *TMS*'s best-loved characters – Brian Johnston, Henry Blofeld, Bill Frindall, Christopher Martin-Jenkins, Fred Trueman, Don Mosey and the one who somehow held it all together – producer Peter Baxter.

AGGERS ON BRIAN JOHNSTON

I applied for the role of BBC cricket correspondent in 1991 after my brief spell at the *Today* newspaper. Mike Lewis, head of sport and outside broadcasts, gave me the job and I was then interviewed again by some people at BBC Sport, fielding questions like: 'How does it feel to be part of *TMS*? You must be thrilled – crikey, think of the footsteps you're following.' I hadn't listened to the programme much after I left home because I was always playing. And so I just thought, er . . . really? So I turned up on the first day of that summer's opening Test against the West Indies, excited and nervous, yes, but not in any way intimidated or anxious about what I was getting into.

The first person I met was Henry Blofeld, who was going the other way to join Sky. We wished each other luck and he then gave me the greatest piece of cricket broadcasting advice ever, which was: 'Don't try and copy anybody.' He was so right. In my first months in the job, I hoovered up any guidance I could get from experienced colleagues and Brian was always ready to help. He passed on the crucial tip that watching the way a player walks is the best way to identify him from distance. He also cautioned that there would always be one completely anonymous fielder who floated around different positions. As long as you'd got everyone else you could usually name him if he pulled off a catch but as a fallback strategy you could just say 'brilliant catch' and then switch commentary to the dismissed batsman while you waited for the fielder's name to flash up on the TV monitor. Tony Cozier's top tip was to say the batsman's name as the bowler runs in because it's always tricky to distinguish between players wearing helmets. By regularly repeating the name of the player facing, you were more likely to get things right. It helped your fluency and was a rhythmical, tidy way of commentating.

Arriving in the Headingley commentary box for that first Test – which England, unusually against the West Indies, won quite comfortably – I found Johnners who immediately turned, smiling, and said: 'Ah, it's Aggers.' That was the first time I'd ever been called that. My nickname at school and throughout my playing career had always been Aggy. But there was little point in persuading Brian of that and, of course, Aggers stuck. I didn't know it then, but Johnners was the best mentor a fledgling broadcaster could ever have hoped for. He was a natural communicator, he had an amazing voice, he could think fast through the unexpected and there was no-one better at keeping listeners entertained through rain breaks. Watching him in action was an education.

You have to remember that times have changed hugely. In the early days, there were no emails, texts or tweets and we had to rely on the hundreds of letters sent to *TMS* to provide a bit of padding during those breaks. Brian alone would get 50 a day and you'd see him in front of the microphone, scorecard in one hand, letter in the other. If he got stuck he'd just quote something from the letter and turn it into a talking point. It was so important because you might have to talk for a very long time. These days it's much easier to fill a break with all the interaction from listeners through social media. There's more on Brian in Chapter 12 because so much of our professional relationship revolved around wind-ups and the joy of each other's live, on-air bloopers. Most of the latter were definitely his.

AGGERS ON DON MOSEY
AND FRED TRUEMAN

Shortly after meeting Johnners, I noticed a load of boxes had been delivered to the commentary box. These contained copies of a book written by one of the *TMS* commentators, the cricket writer Don Mosey, titled *The Alderman's Tale*. Don had been nicknamed 'The Alderman' by Brian on the basis that he looked like Brian's idea of a town mayor. The books had been stacked in place by Don's publisher ready for him to sign. Unbeknown to me, I was entering the commentary box at a somewhat delicate moment.

More of these books arrived at every Test venue that summer and it soon became clear to me that they should all have been stamped 'AWKWARD'. The problem was that Don had taken a sledgehammer to everybody on *TMS*, but particularly Christopher Martin-Jenkins and Peter Baxter. It was dreadful. Peter was the programme's producer, after all. Don suspected that 1991 would be his last year at *TMS* and he was going to get the bullet. So he thought he'd bring out his book while he had the chance. It followed us everywhere and created serious tension. Don was a strange old boy, a bit chippy and convinced the world was against him. He called me aside on that first day, saying: 'I want to let you know, Jonathan, that just because you went to public school, I won't hold it against you.' I thanked him, thinking, 'What a very strange man.'

Things reached a head on the eve of the 4th Test at Edgbaston. Mike Lewis had arranged a kind of clear-the-air dinner just up the road at Pebble Mill. The England coach Micky Stewart was special guest and most of the *TMS* regulars, including Fred Trueman, were there. But it proved a disaster. At one point, somebody mischievously lobbed in the question: 'It seems extraordinary to me, Fred, that you're not involved in the England coaching set-up.' This was a well-trodden way to light Fred's blue touchpaper. Indeed I always dreaded taking over the *TMS* mic from the Australian sports commentator Neville Oliver if Fred was alongside summarising. Neville would delight in handing over with the words: 'Fred, I can't believe you're not coaching England, mate . . . now here's Jonathan Agnew,' and then I'd have Fred muttering and combusting next to me for the next half-hour. Yet, make no mistake, I loved Fred. If he was summarising I used to look forward to rain breaks because you got to hear loads of his extraordinary cricketing stories. He would never take the mickey out of himself but he could make you laugh even when he was angry and chuntering away. He just had one of those faces.

The Pebble Mill dinner soon descended into a heated argument between Fred and Micky on England's coaching strategy. It culminated in Micky offering Fred the chance to 'go outside and settle it'. He threw open a door, which unfortunately – or perhaps fortunately – turned out to be a broom cupboard. Mike tried to soothe things by proposing the Loyal Toast only for that to spark another row as BBC cricket reporter Pat Murphy, an avowed republican, declined to participate. This deeply upset Johnners, who strongly supported the monarchy, and the night ended with the real possibility that Johnners might quit *TMS*. We were soon all back behind the microphone and the usual banter resumed. But that evening illustrated the reality of life on *TMS*. There's a notion that we're all close friends and spend all our time together. But we're all different people, different ages, different interests. We might go out for a meal during a Test but we're just like anyone else socialising with work colleagues.

NICE LINE
Fiery Fred Trueman

Yorkshireman Fred Trueman was unquestionably one of England's all-time great fast bowlers with 307 Test and over 2300 first-class wickets to his name. He was fearsome in his verbal assessment of batters and had a habit of popping into his opponents' dressing room before the start of play to advise who would be among his victims. There were invariably plenty of candidates. When his autobiography was almost finished his publisher asked if he had any ideas for a title. Trueman volunteered: 'The Definitive Volume on the Finest Bloody Fast Bowler That Ever Drew Breath'.

The former Somerset player turned umpire Ken Palmer once told how he was batting with his captain Harold Stephenson when, in the midst of a Trueman over, Stephenson called Palmer over to say: 'Ken, just tell Trueman to remove that bit of paper that's blowing about at the back of him.' Nervously, Palmer approached the great man to pass on this request. Trueman stared at him, then Stephenson, with disdain. 'Well, just go and ask your skipper who the 'ell he thinks I am. Tell 'im I'm not the Corporation dustman.'

AGGERS ON BILL FRINDALL

Bill was an interesting character because he was a frustrated broadcaster. He'd been doing the *TMS* scorer's job for years when I started and at that time we all had open microphones set up on the table. However, our producer Peter Baxter got so fed up with Bill's snorts and grunts and interferences that eventually he insisted on him using a lip mic. Not only did Bill then have to pick it up to speak, he had to press a switch as well. I remember him turning up on the first day of the new regime. He was completely crestfallen, devastated. As he saw it, his vital contributions to the *TMS* coverage had been summarily cast aside.

It's easy to forget just how good Bill was. He would provide incredible statistical information at a time when the World Wide Web hadn't even been invented. He had a mysterious system involving blue and red colour-coded volumes, and it must have worked because he knew exactly where to find most things, most of the time. His reference books and folders would be lugged around on one of those railway station porters' trolleys, carefully lashed into place, and then dragged upstairs to some cramped commentary box where he would immediately commandeer half the space. He also had three old analogue stopwatches fixed to a board. They were arranged in front of him so that the ones on the left and right represented the time the respective batsmen had been at the crease while the centre one showed the length of their partnership. Two would therefore be reset whenever a wicket fell. However, Bill treated these timings as privileged information

which was strictly his to announce, a way of getting his voice on
the radio.

He was a particularly aggressive fast bowler in club cricket and I
imagine as eccentric on the field as he was off it. His wife Debbie, or
Debbers as he always called her, would prepare these amazing meals
for his lunch and tea in the *TMS* box. He was big on seafood,
especially crayfish and mussels served with a healthy salad. At Lord's,
you'd see Johnners tucking in to roast beef sandwiches made
specially by the Middlesex cook Nancy (see Chapter 4), Bill peeling a
prawn or something and the rest of us staring down at cold ham and
cheese and biscuits delivered in an airline box.

Without being unkind to him, Bill saw his job as the most important
on *Test Match Special* and so it was only right that he had the most
room. He took the role very seriously, although he had a good sense
of humour and listeners would often hear him laughing – especially
at any innuendos or double entendres that cropped up in
commentary. Indeed, it was his snort of laughter that made the
infamous Botham 'Legover' commentary go on for quite so long
(see Chapter 12).

He pretty much invented modern-day scoring, his scorebooks were
a work of art and he became a cornerstone of *TMS*. But he'd guard
his books jealously like a schoolboy doing his homework with a free
hand tucked tightly around the paper so you couldn't see what he
was writing. He was always hoping for the chance to correct you on
air. You'd ask him for information with your hand over the mic and
he'd pretend not to hear. So you'd say to the listeners, 'I think the

batsman's on six,' whereupon Bill would quickly switch on his mic and say: 'It's seven, actually.' He was a bit of a monkey like that. When the clock was ticking towards the end of a programme and you had the Shipping Forecast coming up and 20 seconds to deliver a summary, you might ask: 'Bill, could you give me the bowling figures?' If he hadn't done them perfectly he would just ignore you. On the whole, though, he was always kind to me. Identification of players is always the hardest thing and we all make mistakes. Bill would usually quietly correct me off-mic. But he was never very generous to Henry Blofeld, whose mistakes would be challenged quickly and sometimes scathingly. They were never the closest allies.

If you contrast Bill with our more recent scorers, Andrew Samson and Andy Zaltzman, the most obvious difference is that their writing is horrendous. Samson's grasp of stats is brilliant. His mind is incredible. He often doesn't even need to look things up because he just knows the answer. But those answers are usually delivered in the form of a totally illegible scrawl on a torn, tatty bit of paper. Zaltzman has brought a fresh look to the role. He particularly shines at stats analysis as well as being the most naturally funny of the three.

AGGERS ON HENRY BLOFELD

Henry was the most amazing commentator I ever worked with. He wasn't there when I arrived on *TMS* – he'd gone to Sky – but then, in 1994, Brian Johnston died. Peter Baxter felt he shouldn't bring Henry straight back as some kind of replacement for Brian, although he was in a way. The first day we all worked together, CMJ tapped me on the shoulder, pointing under the table, and as Henry started commentating you could see his feet tapping madly in some kind of bizarre, seated dance. He is this absolute force of energy, the most incredibly colourful, energetic commentator ever. Every ball is an event. His voice, his descriptive talents, the stories he tells – any commentary team is stronger with Henry in it but, sadly, once he was diagnosed with macular degeneration it became impossible for him to see a cricket ball 100 yards away.

He never said no to work. He was insatiable in the way he hoovered it up and that's because he loved it. When in 1998 the Sabina Park Test in Jamaica was abandoned, we in the media headed for the outfield to try and establish what was going on. I needed a quick pee first and arrived in the only toilet cubicle to find Henry already in there giving an animated live commentary to a radio station somewhere in the world. I'm not sure what the listeners made of the sound of me flushing the loo next to him.

On his last day at *TMS* in 2017 he did an entirely unplanned lap of honour at Lord's. It was never meant to be like that. When a game ends, I usually walk around to the pavilion to interview players and this time Peter suggested I take Henry and summariser Vic Marks with me. Henry didn't realise what was going on until we got to the Mound Stand when spectators immediately clocked who he was, largely because of the absurd pastels, yellows, greens and oranges which constituted his clobber that day, and began cheering him like a hero. Henry, of course, responded and I started commentating on the scene. We got halfway round the ground to find the players weren't ready so I suggested – knowing what the answer would be – 'Come on, Henry, do you fancy doing the other half?' So off we went around the Warner Stand and the Grand Stand, and there was just this tsunami of goodwill raining down on him. It was incredible. And then we had to do the first half all over again. If you compare his *TMS* retirement to that of John Arlott – who simply said: 'Now it's over to Christopher Martin-Jenkins' – well, Henry was never going to go out like that.

Our *TMS* team selection has to be canny and has to have depth. Those of us who have been around a long time, you hope, have got that depth and can be resourceful and commentate in a way that works. But for your 20-minute stint you're a caricature of what you are. You couldn't talk like it in real life – Blowers would combust if that were the case. You sit down, take the microphone, take a deep breath, your brain is going incredibly fast, you've got no script and you have to be on it, absolutely wired to the game.

What we call the 'thread' of the show is all-important. *TMS* is, above all, ball-by-ball commentary and sometimes I tell summarisers off for talking too long as the bowler is running in. You don't want that. Most listeners can't be at the venue and they need a picture painted that puts them in the moment. Of course, Blowers was brilliant at that. He'd talk of the bowler running in, limbs pumping, hair swept back, all that vital colour which brings a scene to life.

AGGERS ON CHRISTOPHER MARTIN-JENKINS

My predecessor as BBC cricket correspondent, the late Christopher Martin-Jenkins, was a lovely man who was an absolutely incurable technophile. He was always having new laptops delivered. He bought one from Marks & Spencer on the way to a game in Cardiff once purely on the grounds that it might be better than his last one. He'd spend hours setting these PCs up, inevitably accompanied by his version of swearing – he was obsessed with never swearing on air so he always used words such as 'fishcakes' or 'Fotheringhay'.

There was a much-celebrated CMJ incident on the 1997–8 West Indies tour which started in Montego Bay. Our colleague Mike Selvey was driving us to the match over the Blue Mountains when Christopher remembered he had to call his sports editor urgently. For some minutes, all we heard from the back seat was 'Fishcakes and Fotheringhay, I can't get through, no signal,' until finally someone noticed that he was trying to dial in on his hotel room TV remote.

CMJ also had a well-earned reputation for being accident prone. In Barbados, he borrowed golf clubs from the president of a local cricket association, hired a Mini Moke and set off for the Royal Westmoreland golf club. After playing his round, and invariably spluttering 'Fotheringhay' as he hacked his way around the bunkers, he tossed the borrowed clubs in the back and returned to his hotel only to find that, en route, a combination of nasty potholes and his driving had resulted in the clubs being scattered across the island behind him. Not one had survived the journey. He had to go on local radio the following day and plead for anyone who found one lying in a bush to return it. He never did get any back. CMJ was a walking calamity. And yet behind the microphone he was the most measured, thoughtful commentator. That was the interesting dichotomy.

NICE LINE

Johnners the war hero

Brian Johnston portrayed himself – correctly – on *TMS* as a genial, innocuous character, so it is sometimes overlooked that he was awarded the Military Cross during the Second World War. This is the third highest decoration that can be bestowed on a member of the British armed forces, awarded for 'an act or acts of exemplary gallantry during active operations against the enemy'. Brian served as a technical adjutant with the 2nd Battalion, The Grenadier Guards, and landed at Arromanches, Normandy, three weeks after the Allies main D-Day assault. By the winter of 1944 his armoured division was in the midst of intense fighting across the Rhineland where his job was to rescue and recover damaged tanks, often under fire. All too often, this meant pulling out horribly injured crews in the hope of finding rapid medical attention. He recounted the horror of it all briefly in his autobiography but resolutely played down the significance of his medal in conversation. It was, he liked to say, 'more or less given out with the rations'.

AGGERS ON THE PRODUCERS – PETER BAXTER AND SHILPA PATEL

Peter Baxter was the engine room behind *TMS*. He had to think for everyone, work with the technicians, plan the programmes and keep an eye on the budget. On foreign tours, we were allowed one free phone call home per week, which I found hard to start with especially as I had two young kids. I'd always make my one call from the commentary box and be aware of Peter looking at his watch. But it wasn't a big deal. We were always close and later became best men at each other's weddings.

We always tried to get a guest in to help see us through breaks in play, and occasionally the prospect of no guest and nothing to say was terrifying. During the 2005 Ashes, the last Test at the Oval when it was all kicking off on the final afternoon, I handed to the news, turned to Peter and asked what we were doing for the tea break. Back came the response: 'Don't know.' I just had no idea what I was going to say. Desperately trying to think of something vaguely meaningful, I suddenly felt a flurry of activity and there, landing in the chair beside me, was none other than Hugh Grant. I've never been so pleased to see someone. Once again, we had been saved by our incredible fixer Shilpa Patel, who had spotted him in the stands at the start of the match and had been working on him for days to get him on. Thank God she succeeded.

Shilpa was Peter's assistant and her great gift was the ability to persuade well-known people sitting in the stands to come on *TMS*. She managed it with a mixture of charm and dogged determination and we would measure guests on how long it took

Shilpa to sign them up. The Queen guitarist Brian May was a three-dayer – even though he was sitting right next to the commentary box. But Shilpa's greatest coup was the New Zealand actor Russell Crowe who was at Lord's for the 2009 Ashes Test as the guest of his cousin Jeff Crowe, the match referee and former Black Caps skipper.

Shilpa had spotted him in the MCC chief executive's box in the Grand Stand – one of her most profitable recruiting venues – and quickly made her pitch, which was equally quickly rebuffed with a commonly used two-word expression. She returned to the commentary box looking very deflated and asking what to do. 'Get back there, Shilpa,' I said. 'He probably doesn't mean it.' Shilpa was a tiny girl, barely eight stone, while Russell was obviously this great bear of a man. But she did it and twenty minutes later he walked into the commentary box. I introduced him as our special *TMS* guest, the first cousin of the match referee.

During every Test we have our 'View from the Boundary' feature when it's just you and your interviewee, live, for 25 minutes. I can't think of any comparable slot in radio broadcasting anywhere – they've all got travel news or weather forecasts or other contributors breaking in. So you are completely at the mercy of your guest. For the 5th Ashes Test at the Oval in 2015 I was due to be joined by Martin Kemp, the actor and former Spandau Ballet bass guitarist. At around 12.30 word came through that he wasn't well and couldn't come on. We had half-an-hour to hunt down a replacement and that task fell to Henry Moeran, who had by now taken over Shilpa's job. Henry had been scurrying frantically around the Oval and at 12.50 he burst into the commentary box to blurt out: 'Great news. It's Davina McCall.' I thought I knew the name but, if I'm honest, I'm not always terribly up on the celebrity world. So I had ten minutes on Wikipedia to try and prepare myself for 25 minutes with Davina.

She came on, she was lovely, delightful, but it took only a few moments to establish she knew absolutely nothing about cricket. Which meant we had to talk about her and I had to wing it. In the course of my ten-minute research, I'd discovered she'd performed some incredible triathlon feat in which she had swum, cycled and run from Scotland to Birmingham. So I ventured: 'Come on, Davina, you're hiding your sporting prowess under your bushel.' Admittedly, this was a slight variation of the phrase hiding your light under a bushel, but I felt it worked OK. She looked at me quizzically, straight in the face, and asked innocently: 'Under my bush?' It was the way she said it and the way she looked. She knew exactly what she was doing. It was the first time since 'The Legover' that I felt a hideous eruption of giggles starting inside and I thought, 'You madam! I really mustn't laugh at this. It would sound so bad.' I started sweating and there was a kind of stifled spluttering but I did hold it together. And we got on like a house on fire after that. She was an absolute star.

Johnners did many a 'View from the Boundary' over the years and his final one, during the 6th Ashes Test at the Oval in August 1993, was his final stint for *TMS*. He interviewed the actor, comedian and music hall historian Roy Hudd and together they sang 'Underneath the Arches'. This was one of Johnners' party pieces during the war – he regarded himself as something of an entertainer for the troops – and everyone gathered in the commentary box to listen. I suspect it would have been one of the highlights of Johnners' whole career. Sadly, not long after this, he suffered a heart attack and died in January 1994 aged 81.

One final word on the commentary box team. When Peter Baxter retired, and Adam Mountford became our producer, it was a changing-of-the-guard moment for *TMS*. This was partly because they had different styles – Peter tended to operate in the background, talking to people, doing rotas and keeping half an ear on us, whereas Adam is much more hands-on, listens to every word and flags up suggestions. But the change has also been one of real substance. Adam came in with two quite challenging tasks: firstly to make the show more diverse and secondly to give it a harder topical edge. If you had done a team photo of the *TMS* broadcasters when I first joined you'd have seen a line-up of white men, all of a similar age apart from myself, which didn't properly reflect modern-day cricket. Now we have great male and female broadcasters from all ethnic backgrounds who can speak with authority on both the men's and women's game.

Adam's other key role was to make our programme 'newsier'. Years ago, we didn't broadcast during intervals in play but now this is integral to *TMS* and it means there's more airtime to fill. As a result we have guests who speak on topical cricket issues, rather than simply being chatty, and we regularly set the cricket news agenda. I should also say that Shilpa, a huge loss when she left the show, has been ably replaced by Henry, who is blessed with her ability to seek and find guests attending Test matches and persuade them to come on *TMS*. I would certainly be lost without his pre-interview briefings because sometimes these star names just pass me by. Henry is also an excellent commentator in his own right and I predict we'll hear a lot more of him behind the microphone in years to come.

Favourite cake

AGGERS Lemon drizzle.

TUFFERS Lemon drizzle. We get loads in the *TMS* box, which are all lovely. Although my favourite ever *TMS* cake was one fashioned professionally for an Ashes Test. It was a kangaroo on all fours in a submissive pose with a rampant male lion behind it doing what lions do. That was a cake to remember.

ISA My BBC Sport colleague Ellie Oldroyd bakes a sumptuous lemon drizzle cake and that does the job for me.

EBONY Angel cake. Those three-layer sponges, pink, yellow and plain. I'd turn up to Young England training with four of them in my kit bag and get a rollocking from the nutritionist. I lived on angel cake for years but I've never seen one arrive in the *TMS* box. Kind listeners, please note.

CARLOS Salted caramel.

ALISON Chocolate, although I'm partial to a good fruit cake too.

AATIF Salted caramel cheesecake with Lotus Biscoff. I'm still waiting for one to arrive in the *TMS* box.

CHAPTER 10

BOX SEATS

In which the team recall a collection of their favourite behind-the-scenes anecdotes – funny, awkward and occasionally deeply touching.

TUFFERS

In 2003, after retiring from professional cricket, I won *I'm a Celebrity . . . Get Me Out of Here* and – perhaps because he thought six weeks in the jungle was useful preparation – the *TMS* producer Adam Mountford invited me to have a go in the commentary box. I didn't need much persuading. Talking about cricket is the next best thing to playing it and, given the occasional grim days I've had on a cricket field, sometimes even better. The first time on air, I was nervous but spin bowlers need to have a good cricket brain because you're always thinking for everyone else. That stood me in good stead. And, of course, the whole team was friendly and didn't try to complicate the job. The key tip was to be yourself and say what you see, which got the best out of me. Aggers gave me loads of support. He's a great mate of mine and still offers advice.

Listeners seemed to enjoy the contrast between myself and the much-loved, but occasionally unworldly, members of the *TMS* team. One of my great pleasures would be to gently probe Henry Blofeld on his lifestyle. A simple question of what he'd had for dinner would elicit very detailed responses on the excellent lobster he'd enjoyed in his hotel room the previous evening. That is *TMS*. It's not all about cricket. It's the characters doing the broadcasting. I remember once during a rain break we were discussing people and businesses with appropriate names, like the fictional solicitors' firm Sue, Grabbit and Runne invented by *Private Eye*. My contribution was to suggest a popular parlour game to Christopher Martin-Jenkins in which he could establish his 'rock star' moniker by combining his mother's maiden name with that of his favourite pet. 'So, you see, Christopher,' I explained encouragingly, 'mine would be Mason Trooper.' CMJ didn't see. 'Well,' he replied cautiously, 'I did once have a cocker spaniel called Rambler.'

The listeners completely buy into this sort of banter and it's what makes *TMS* their programme. Not just their tweets and emails on cricket matters, important though these are, but the way they respond to issues we raise. Sometimes they even get actively involved in the nuts-and-bolts of the show, such as when I mentioned how my headphones got awfully sweaty and caused me to suffer itchy ears. A couple of days later, a woman very kindly sent in two sets of elasticated cotton ear-protectors to keep the cans off my skin. They are known as Tuffers' Muffers and 12 years later they remain in full working order. I keep a pair and Adam Mountford has the spare set. That listener has made my life in the commentary box a whole lot more comfortable.

On the morning of a game, I'm cautious about engaging players in conversation if I'm out doing a pitch report. If bowlers are marking out their run, we'll maybe exchange a few words and if their team is 3–0 up in the series they're likely to be quite chatty. Occasionally they might even ask for my thoughts on the pitch. But if there's a big toss to be won or a tough day ahead, it's usually just a nod and everyone goes about their business. Fortunately, I can leave the trickier stuff to Aggers. On days when the fielding team has been battered for hundreds of runs or the batting side has folded for 40-odd, then he's the one going out with his microphone at the end of play to ask for their thoughts on an omnishambles. We have to get reaction to the bad as well as the good. The one thing in our favour is that attitudes to the press and media have changed since I was a player. Today's players realise we're not out to nail them, we want the England team to do well, and the fact that many of us are ex-players has helped that change.

One particular *TMS* pitch report, actually nothing to do with the pitch, stands out in my memory. On the eve of the England–South Africa 3rd Test at the Oval in 2017, Graham Gooch and I were asked to present England caps to three players who were making their debut – Tom Westley, Dawid Malan and Toby Roland-Jones. It was agreed that Graham would do Tom Westley, who was an Essex lad, and I'd do the others, who were both Middlesex boys. This isn't the sort of thing I particularly enjoy doing but I said I'd be delighted and then spent a restless night going through what I hoped would be a Churchillian speech which the whole team would hear as they gathered around.

The following day, I'd just finished doing my *TMS* bit and was glancing across to the England team waiting for my cue to enter their huddle and deliver my crafted words of wisdom from a sheaf of notes. Goochie was there as well and as soon as we got the nod he asked if he could go first. Which was fine by me. Graham then delivered this epic speech telling Tom what a privilege it was to play for his country, how he'd made his parents proud, how he'd worked so hard and so on. Meanwhile, I'm standing behind him crossing out the same lines – which in fairness were a tad clichéd – that I'd scribbled down.

By the time it was my turn, I'd not got a new line left. I handed out the caps, congratulated Dawid and Toby, took a deep breath and offered only: 'What a wonderful day to be alive.' It was certainly a wonderful debut for Toby because when he was brought on to bowl the following day, he managed, in the space of 33 balls, to take the wickets of South Africa's top four batters – Dean Elgar, Heino Kuhn, Quinton de Kock and the biggest prize, Hashim Amla, who had made 311 not out during his last Test at the Oval. Toby ended with a five-for and I'm happy to claim some of the credit. There is a postscript to all this because, during my first *TMS* stint that morning, I mentioned what had happened. Within a couple of hours some bloke wrote in to say he'd had loads of T-shirts printed with a mocked-up photo of me looking like Che Guevara alongside the words 'What a Wonderful Day to Be Alive'. I never did find out if they sold.

ALISON

My first full commentary game for radio was an Essex v. Northants
county match in 2006 at Chelmsford, the old Pro40 competition,
with former England bowlers Graeme Swann and Alex Tudor sitting
alongside. I felt at home with them because I knew Graeme a little
through my Northants links and I'd done previous broadcasting
work with Alex. By then, I'd covered my first Test match – England v.
South Africa at Lord's in 2003 – for the BBC Asian Network and
had begun working with Adam Mountford, reporting county games
for BBC Radio 5 Live. By the time I did my first England commentary
in September 2007, at the inaugural ICC World Twenty20 in South
Africa, I'd already established myself as a voice of cricket on 5 Live.
I'd travelled to South Africa to cover the 2005 Women's World Cup
and later that year I was on the England men's Test and ODI tour to
Pakistan. I'd also been assigned to the ICC men's World Cup in the
Caribbean in spring 2007, when I found myself thrust into an
unexpected commentary role as Ireland famously upset Pakistan in
Jamaica. So, later that year, it wasn't as though *TMS* had just plucked
a female from nowhere to join the team.

I was, however, very aware that there hadn't been a woman's voice
commentating on *TMS* for nearly ten years. A Barbadian lawyer,
Donna Symmonds, joined the programme as overseas guest
commentator for a number of matches between 1998 and 2000 but
there had never been a woman setting out her stall to be a long-term
career commentator on *TMS*, which was what I wanted to do.
To give an idea of the climate at the time, Jacqui Oatley had made

her debut as a *Match of the Day* football commentator only a few months earlier and the backlash to that had been extreme. There was therefore a lot of nervousness from BBC bosses behind the scenes about the reception a female might get commenting for *TMS* on men's cricket. I always felt ready, I was known and hopefully respected on the circuit, and I'd done the groundwork. But it was still a huge step to be trusted with *TMS* ball-by-ball duties. Not a lot of fuss was made of it because the BBC believed a low-key debut would help me avoid being instantly shot down by the usual suspects. In 2007, we didn't have Twitter but we did have email, which could be bad enough, and you always felt certain newspaper columnists were poised to have a go at certain commentators.

I put myself under so much pressure to avoid making any tiny error, like saying the wrong player's name or misidentifying a fielding position, because I knew someone would jump on that. And it wouldn't have been: 'Alison Mitchell is a poor commentator' but rather: 'Women can't commentate on cricket.' It felt as if I were representing an entire gender, which was of course ridiculous, but very real. When I did that first England commentary in September 2007, I think most listeners thought I'd been commentating internationally for a while anyway, because they were so familiar with my voice through Radio 5 Live and previous work during World Cups. 5 Live would often come to me for little commentary spells during the closing stages of a match. And, crucially, during that 2007 World Cup in the Caribbean, I'd been thrust into the biggest sports story of the time, the death of Bob Woolmer (see Chapter 11).

My most memorable broadcasting moment was the Women's World
Cup final of 2017, definitely a day that had a much wider cultural
significance for the sport in this country, and indeed across the
women's cricketing world. The whole day and occasion felt seminal
for the sport. I was leading the *TMS* commentary team for that final
at Lord's and was on air for the tense final stages and the winning
moment, whereupon my own words are etched into my memory
because they've been played on loop on 5 Live Sports Extra for the
last four years! 'Six wickets for Anya Shrubsole, England's hero –
England win the World Cup!' A highlight in my own commentary
career for sure, and as an occasion, right up there with the men's
Ashes series of 2005, which I reported on for BBC 5 Live and the
BBC Asian Network.

EBONY

I was in the *TMS* commentary box with Aggers and Dan Norcross in September 2018 when Sir Alastair Cook, who had already announced his retirement, signed off at the Oval with a Test century in his final innings. It was a jaw-dropping moment – he was already England's leading Test run-scorer of all time and in that match against India he became the highest-scoring left-hander ever to play Test cricket.

In broadcasting, you're trying to fill every moment. But just before Cook's 100 came up Aggers said to me: 'Don't forget this is history. Your commentary will be repeated for ever. Let the moment breathe.' On 96, Alastair pushes a single to backward point off the bowling of Ravindra Jadeja. It gets fielded by Jasprit Bumrah who, seeing Cook gently jogging along, hurls the ball at the bowler's end stumps in an attempted run out. He misses, no fielder has backed up, the ball races to the boundary and Cook's single becomes a five. It takes a moment for the spectators and ourselves in the *TMS* box to realise what has just happened. Then suddenly everyone in the stadium rises to their feet and this incredible wall of sound and applause wells up.

That went on for two minutes, during which I don't remember us saying anything. Honestly, what needed to be said? It taught me the importance in broadcasting of allowing the impact of the moment. Let history be made and keep quiet.

NICE LINE
Chef on fire

During Sir Alastair Cook's 12-year Test career you could be forgiven for thinking he was on a personal crusade to rewrite records. Since he was summoned from an ECB academy tour in the West Indies to assist an injury-stricken senior England team in 2006 (he promptly scored a debut century in Nagpur), he has blossomed into a run machine of rare vintage. By the time he retired in 2018 he was England's leading scorer with 12,472 runs, the most prolific left-hander in Test history and the player who has appeared in more consecutive Tests (159) than any other. The opener nicknamed 'Chef' – for obvious reasons – also had a distinguished stint as his country's captain, winning 24 out of 59 matches to become England's second most successful skipper behind Michael Vaughan, who won 26.

AGGERS

Helping new members of the team is part of my role on *Test Match Special*. I suppose I'm the senior pro and I've been fortunate enough to see and commentate on a lot of cricket. If you're on the microphone at one of those big, landmark moments in the game, it is intimidating and you can wreck it if you're not careful. It's particularly hard for the summariser, as Ebony was for that Alastair Cook century, to keep quiet. You don't want to gabble or you'll spoil the moment. I see it as my job to put someone at ease but also to make sure they know they're involved in something very special and pass on a thought about how to do it. A huge crowd, Cook scoring a century like that – there's almost no need to say anything. But if you do, then bear in mind that while you may be the soloist the crowd is your orchestral backing. And you have to find the right melody in your voice.

If you're commentating on a match in my style, you venture anywhere. There are other commentators whose style is much straighter and focused purely on cricket, which is also fine because our main job is to describe the game. But I tend to go with the flow and throw random thoughts around. That means I'll sometimes forget a name or forget a place and Adam will say it in my ear or someone will shout out from the back of the box. But I'd rather that sense of unpredictability. I never work to a script and if I see someone with loads of notes it's slightly troubling because you fear they're just going to read them out. The only script I ever have is at the end of the show when Adam will put on the screen what's coming up later in the evening.

Sometimes you have to deal with the unplanned and the unpredictable. Bad language on air is always a big no-no and I once had a tricky exchange with the legendary Aussie fast bowler Jeff Thomson when he first appeared on *TMS* as an Ashes summariser. Inside ten minutes, and in a perfectly friendly way, Thommo slipped in two buggers and a bastard. Fortunately, we were still on Radio 4 then and as we approached lunch I was able to hurriedly hand over to the Shipping Forecast. That meant we were still broadcasting to Australia but not to the UK and I was able to say on air: 'Look, Thommo old chap, it might be OK for our audience in Australia but would you mind toning down the language?' And he did. He was as good as gold after that.

EBONY

I've also fallen into the fruity-language trap. My first overseas trip for *TMS* was England's October 2016 tour to Bangladesh. I can't remember the match but I was taking in the atmosphere and daydreaming when Aggers suddenly asked: 'What do you think, Ebony?' I mean, what did I think about what? I obviously couldn't say that so I broadcast to the nation the first words which came into my head. Which were: 'Do you know what, just twat it.' The truth is that all players from club to Test level would have recognised 'twat' as a cricketing term to describe a well-struck shot. I just didn't think about its literal meaning. Aggers managed to gloss over it but after our stint on commentary I got a severe telling-off from Adam. I learned a lot from that and I now mentally flick a switch when I'm broadcasting to avoid any controversial phrases.

ISA

There are moments in broadcasting when it's hard to avoid getting caught up in the moment and that can be a pitfall. For me, Australia winning the T20 World Cup in Melbourne in March 2020, and the significance of that day for women's cricket and women's sport in general, was one of those pitfall moments. To think that 86,000 people turned up for that game and it produced the best viewer ratings ever for a women's cricket match. It was a win for women's sport and for all those that had gone before to get us to that point.

Katy Perry was opening and closing a show for TV and I was down on the boundary with Mel Jones and Alex Blackwell to give our insight into proceedings. At one point we were stood there, open-mouthed, just watching the performance unfold before suddenly realising we were live on camera treating viewers to the sight of us watching the cricket.

AGGERS

As a commentator and cricket correspondent, your relationship with the players is inevitably edgy at times. You're not a cheerleader and if things aren't going well you need to be critical. That can lead to a sulky response from one or two. I remember a particularly awkward encounter with Steve Harmison after he bowled that shocker of a wide delivery to kick off the 2006–7 Ashes tour in Brisbane. The media reaction was not good and a few days later I entered a lift to find that he and I were the only people going down ten storeys. It was awfully uncomfortable, and what can you say: I think it was 'Hi, Steve', 'Hi, Aggers', and that was the extent of the conversation. It's no coincidence that the happiest tour I ever had was when England won the 2010–11 Ashes. Everyone enjoyed it, both players and media, but it's a different world when the team is losing. I do think more experienced players recognise that we have to be honest in this job and tell it like it is. If you don't, no-one will ever believe a word you say.

The 4th Test at Barbados during the West Indies 1994 tour was another good example of tetchy relations. It was one of the unlikeliest England wins I've ever seen, achieved on a ground where the record showed it was almost impossible for any touring side to win; the previous occasion was in 1935. Alec Stewart got two hundreds, Gus Fraser bowled brilliantly to take 8–75, Andy Caddick got a five-for, Tuffers took a fantastic catch that got Lara out, running backwards, and all of us in the press were genuinely thrilled that England had won the game. But they had lost their previous

seven Test matches and had looked ordinary in a warm-up against
the West Indies Board XI. So criticism had been building and as a
result the players developed a siege mentality in which they viewed
the media as the enemy. When I walked past their dressing room
door to follow Michael Atherton into his press conference, I heard
Gus Fraser yell: 'Give 'em f*** all, Mike.' Atherton wasn't quite so
unforgiving but his response to one question said it all: 'Our victory
rates as a very sweet moment for me.'

The following Test in Antigua was, thanks to Brian Lara's record 375
score, one of *the* moments of my *TMS* career. If I know we're
nearing some cricketing landmark like that, I always write a line in
my notebook in advance in case I happen to be on air when it
happens. I find this helps me lodge an appropriate response in my
memory. However, the closer we got to that 375 target the clearer it
became from the rota that it wouldn't be me at the microphone. The
job was much more likely to fall to Vic Marks. Victor then came
over to me, ashen-faced, and said: 'Oh Lord, it could be on my stint.
Would you mind doing it for me?' To which I said: 'Look, just do it.
Write yourself a line and get it in your head.' In fact, the stroke that
secured the record happened on Christopher Martin-Jenkins' watch,
although I felt the most perceptive remark came from Trevor Bailey.
who very rarely embellished or exaggerated anything he saw on a
cricket field. He turned to me on air and said: 'Let's be honest,
Jonathan. If the outfield had been cut properly he'd have scored
450.' And he was right because the grass was so long. Lara was
a man on a mission. He had the shots, he had the time and no-one –
certainly not England – was going to stop him.

The moment he reached the record a wave of sheer happiness engulfed the ground. People were running on to the outfield doing cartwheels and somersaults. Crowds were everywhere, Gary Sobers was wandering around, charming as ever, and Chickie's Disco was blaring out some party tunes. And, to make this scene even more surreal, one of my mates, a British Airways pilot, then brought his jumbo jet in on his final approach to Antigua airport, which is just beyond the St John's ground, at less than 1000 feet. It was an incredible noise and he was low enough to be off the radar. He got a bollocking for it from his bosses but it was all perfectly safe. He appeared in the commentary box an hour or so later with a cake from Marks & Spencer.

Lara was magnificent that day but one of the greatest innings I ever witnessed was Atherton's 185 not out in the 2nd Test at the Wanderers, Johannesburg, the following year. This came on England's first tour to South Africa following the end of apartheid. It was a defiant, courageous innings lasting 643 minutes and 492 balls. It was played against two world-class fast bowlers in Allan Donald and Shaun Pollock. And it started with both the South African crowd and the fielders being noisy, aggressive and very confident they were going to win. What struck me was how that noise melted away as Atherton ruthlessly snuffed out the attack. England had been set 479 to win when South Africa captain Hansie Cronje declared at lunch on the fourth day. There was a feeling he'd batted on too long so that Brian McMillan could get a century but, even so, there was over a day-and-a-half left in the game. Atherton, ably assisted by Jack Russell, who himself stood firm for four-and-a-half hours, duly secured the draw and afterwards it fell to me to interview Hansie in front of the whole press. I always got on well with him so I mildly asked whether he perhaps might have declared a bit earlier? He didn't take that well. He literally snatched the microphone out of my hand and gave me the most awesome bollocking on the lines of 'absolutely not, that's a disgraceful suggestion'. He was very agitated about not winning.

On a lighter note, the match also presented a perfect opportunity for some Geoffrey Boycott baiting. Atherton had passed 100 and *TMS* had briefly gone off air for the Shipping Forecast. But Geoffrey, who was summarising for us, had wandered into the commentary box unaware of that and thinking we were still live. So I waded in: 'Look at Atherton, Geoffrey. He's absolutely brilliant. Let's face it, whenever you were batting you sent everyone off to the bars. You used to bore people rigid.' On and on I went. He couldn't hit back because I was still commentating and he thought we were broadcasting.

When on tour with *TMS* I tend to stay in the same hotel as the players every other game. They don't want to see me all the time and I feel the same about them. No-one wants to constantly hang around with work colleagues. In recent years, Joe Root has introduced a brilliant tour innovation which he calls an 'England Night'. The players throw some money into a pot which goes to charity and they invite all members of the press who have played for England. For that night, you feel back in the fold. It's very cleverly done; for instance, in Hamilton, New Zealand, during the 2019 tour we had a cricket quiz night with questions relevant to all generations. Ollie Pope was my captain – I still call him skipper when I see him.

Part of the beauty of it is that players are reminded that they're only in the limelight for a while. And that, one day, they too may work in the media. Chatting to Jofra Archer, I realised he saw me purely as a reporter with a microphone and had no idea I'd played for England. That didn't bother me in the slightest but I do like the fact that players know my background. I feel that when I ask them questions they're more able to respect my role because inside everyone who has played for England there's a fierce pride at having done it. That same evening I had a beer with Zak Crawley – this was the eve of his Test debut – and it was great to sit and talk to him as a player rather than an interviewer.

AATIF

I had a dreamlike *TMS* debut. It was in 2020 during the COVID pandemic, under lock and key inside a bubble at the Ageas Bowl, Southampton. We were in a hotel populated only by the Pakistan squad, the England squad, their support teams, hotel staff, umpires and then all these legends of cricket working in the media. The likes of Michael Holding, Wasim Akram, Shane Warne, Aggers, Tuffers, Michael Vaughan, Isa Guha, Ebony Rainford-Brent and Mark Ramprakash. It was truly bizarre because most of them were having quite a tricky time being thrown together and unable to see their families. Whereas me, I was like a kid locked in a sweetshop. I was surrounded by childhood cricket heroes, chatting to them and even playing cricket with some of them.

On the concourse every night, my fellow *TMS* commentator Henry Moeran, our scorer Andy Zaltzman, producer Adam Mountford and other members of the BBC crew would get together for a knockabout using the floodlight pylons as the wicket. We weren't allowed to do much exercise, and couldn't use the gyms, so this was a handy bit of cardio work. Besides, watching Test cricket all day makes you want to have a go yourself.

One evening Tuffers came down to bowl at me and it was filmed for social media. I can't tell you the number of beautiful cover drives and sweeps I played but the one clip they used was Phil beating the edge of my bat with a proper, turning delivery. So I appealed to Tuffers to give me another chance and we did it all again the next day.

This time he brought Shane Warne and Wasim Akram down with him. Shane was bowling at Adam, found the outside edge and the ball dropped just short of me at slip. That was the one chance in my life to take a catch off Shane. Agony. Mounty then hit Wasim for a lovely boundary, which I doubt will be forgotten any time soon. For obvious reasons, none of this usually happens when *TMS* covers a Test match. It was an amazing two weeks.

TUFFERS

We had a great crew for those lockdown Tests, which is just as well because we were in the secure 'bubbles' for a long time and it all felt a bit weird. We really did feel as though we were providing an important national service and I guess we were. We had so many texts, tweets and emails from people telling us how wonderful it was to listen to *TMS*, and how we were an anchor of normality when everything else was falling apart. Elderly people, shielding, seeing nobody, were telling us that listening to the cricket somehow reassured them that the world wasn't coming to an end – that there was hope and a way forward. It was so heartening and proved to us that the power of radio is undiminished. Sadly, one or two messages from people whose relatives were poorly were very difficult to hear.

AGGERS

It was public service broadcasting – what the BBC is all about – and we were trying our best to bring some normality into people's lives during the lockdown. That's what drove us. Even though there was no background sound, no crowd and it sounded like we were commentating from a toilet, it was necessary to keep the show on the road. It was a reminder that radio is companionship, a friend you take around with you, a gentle voice in the background that talks to you, as opposed to TV broadcasts, which tend to talk at you from a corner of your room.

The pandemic was a unique experience for cricket but we've long known the impact *TMS* can have on our listeners' lives. Perhaps the most poignant letter we have received in my time with the programme came in August 2018 from a chap called Patrick Taylor. Adam handed it me as soon as I walked into the commentary box, saying: 'You have got to read this on air.' In fact, I put it to one side so that by the time I did read it live it was the first time I'd seen it. Patrick talked about the tough time his dad John had been through, a string of illnesses, severe dementia and the fact that he'd been at death's door. Patrick and his wife had gone to visit him in hospital for what they expected to be the final time and his wife had the idea of switching on *TMS* because John was once such a big cricket fan. Within a few minutes, the commentary had brought him round. Patrick was able to talk to him and say goodbye. Woakes scored 100 and John died soon after the game ended. It was all extraordinarily moving and it promoted a big discussion in the media about dementia and the way small things can help.

NICE LINE

Saying goodbye: Patrick Taylor's letter to *TMS*

Patrick wrote how he'd been informed by hospital staff that his cricket-mad father John had 24 to 48 hours to live and might not regain consciousness. As he and his wife sat at John's bedside, she switched on *TMS*. 'After five minutes he opened his eyes,' Patrick wrote. 'He was completely "in the room", able to convey that he was comfortable, he was at peace and I was able to tell him what a wonderful father he is and just how much I love him. Not one comfortable with massive shows of emotion, after 15 minutes he requested that we listen to the cricket. For three hours we listened to Woakes crashing it about at Lord's and making his Test century . . . I don't think that it is any coincidence that he passed peacefully just after England had sealed victory.'

TOP LIST

Best broadcasting moment

AGGERS Without doubt Ben Stokes's Ashes Test innings at Headingley in 2019, the like of which I can say, with absolute certainty, I will never see again.

TUFFERS The World Cup final at Lord's, 14 July 2019, England v. New Zealand. I was summarising for the last half-hour of the game but it then got extended for the tie-breaker Super Overs. It was just as well Aggers was anchoring everything. My contribution was to scream over him things like: 'RUN, RUN' or 'OH NO, WHAT'S HE DOING?' or 'YOU'LL NEVER SEE ANOTHER GAME OF CRICKET LIKE THIS.'

ISA Australia winning the T20 World Cup in Melbourne in March 2020, and the significance of that day for women's cricket and women's sport in general. A huge crowd, fantastic TV ratings – it was a triumph for all the sportswomen who had helped get us to that point.

EBONY September 2018 in the *TMS* commentary box with Aggers and Dan Norcross when Sir Alastair Cook, who had already announced his retirement, signed off at the Oval with a Test century in his final innings. Cricket history unfolding in front of me.

CARLOS During the West Indies Test series at the height of the pandemic lockdown in 2020, I was working for *TMS* and had no idea what was going on when I heard in my headphones that listeners on Radio 4 were leaving us for the Shipping Forecast. What was that all about? Then they let me have a go at reading it myself. Loved it.

ALISON Leading the *TMS* commentary team for the Women's World Cup final at Lord's in 2017. I was on air for the tense final stages and the winning moment, and my words are etched into my memory because they've been played on loop on Radio 5 Live Sports Extra for the last four years! 'Six wickets for Anya Shrubsole, England's hero – England win the World Cup!'

AATIF Being asked off-air by Wasim Akram how I thought an England run chase at Headingley would go during the 2019 World Cup. Here was that guy from the poster on my bedroom wall asking my opinion on a huge game. Priceless.

TOP LIST

Worst broadcasting moment

AGGERS Following the death of the great Australian batsman Lindsay Hassett, we were due to play a tape of his obituary. Instead, we broadcast a brass oompah band.

TUFFERS We're surrounded by such good people at *TMS* that there aren't many of these. I do remember one game I was summarising for Sky at the Oval and observed that a player had 'absolutely twatted the ball through the off side'. I was quickly advised by the producer that this was not a term to use live on TV.

ISA Somewhat bizarrely, this is the same as my best moment. That T20 World Cup win for Australia in 2020. Katy Perry was opening and closing a show for TV and I was down on the boundary with Mel Jones and Alex Blackwell to give our insight into proceedings. At one point we were stood there, open-mouthed, just watching the performance unfold amid the roar of that huge crowd. Then we realised we were live on camera treating viewers to the sight of us watching the cricket.

EBONY I did a Tuffers, I'm afraid. My first overseas trip for *TMS* – England's October 2016 tour to Bangladesh. I was daydreaming during one game when Aggers suddenly asked: 'What do you think, Ebony?' I said the first words that came into my head, which were: 'Do you know what, just twat it.' Nightmare. Aggers managed to gloss over it but after our stint on commentary I got a severe telling-off from our producer Adam.

AATIF When I joined *TMS* there was some social media nonsense from a small minority of haters. Comments like I was only fulfilling a racial quota, I'd never played professional cricket so what did I know? But there were far bigger positives. My comedy is mainly aimed at the immigrant population but thanks to *TMS* I found that white people were suddenly interested in me.

CHAPTER 11

BREAKING NEWS ON *TMS*

In which *TMS* broadcasters find themselves
at the centre of major cricketing news stories.

AGGERS

Over the years, the line between sport and news coverage has become increasingly blurred and at times cricket, with its huge worldwide audience, inevitably ends up as a front-page story. As a live ball-by-ball service, *TMS* can be in the van of a breaking news story and decisions have to be made fast as to how we handle it. The case of Mike Atherton's apparent ball-tampering during the 1st Test against South Africa in 1994 perfectly illustrates the point.

This wasn't any old match. After a 29-year exile during the global fight against apartheid, Nelson Mandela had become President of South Africa and the tourists were finally back playing cricket in England. Surely, everyone would be on their best behaviour, especially the England captain Mike Atherton who was taking the helm at Lord's for his first full home series. However, during the afternoon a cameraman spotted the newbie skipper apparently rubbing dirt from his pocket on to the ball. At the time, cricket watchers were obsessed with ball tampering. Dark suspicion had surrounded the electric performances of Pakistan's bowling duo Waqar Younis and Wasim Akram during their 1992 tour of England, and there was much righteous indignation at suggestions the Pakistanis had discreetly roughened-up one side of the ball. The claim was that this would cause it to 'reverse swing' – you can grow old trying to explain that but, in essence, it is a ball delivered with an action and grip which should make it move *away* from the batsman but actually moves *in*. And vice versa.

At the time Atherton discreetly produced the dirt, the BBC had cut to a horse race. UK viewers were therefore none the wiser. But in South Africa, where the incident *was* shown live, there was uproar. The BBC director decided he would show a recorded clip as soon as terrestrial coverage resumed and so, to introduce that, the live camera zoomed in on Atherton. And as that happened, Athers did it again. Commentator Richie Benaud was caught on the hop and said something bizarre and mysterious like, 'It's strange what you see in the city at night.'

There's no doubt it was one of the most difficult calls of my career as BBC cricket correspondent because it was head-on-the-block stuff. All I know is that the media had been highly energised over Pakistan tampering with the ball and quite right too. But then why should it be any different for the England captain? I had to take a position and I was left with no option. Was I really going to go on TV and say to viewers, 'What you've just seen there, it didn't actually happen'? I couldn't do that.

Perhaps influenced by the ball-tampering rumours, I said on air that he'd been caught and should resign as captain. I took no pleasure in that because he and I had enjoyed a really good relationship up until then. The incident split the media pack and the fallout continues even to this day. The tabloids pretty much sided with me but some of the broadsheets wrote very hostile stuff suggesting I should lose my job for expressing an opinion. Fortunately, the BBC supported me but it was a really unpleasant time. Mike and I have never spoken about it and I wish we could. There are no hard feelings between us but it's the elephant in the room. I enjoy his company, I admire his cricket writing greatly and I'd be interested to know how he would have covered the story because he's a fair-minded man.

Sometimes we're on air as a story breaks elsewhere and our guest summariser just happens to be a key figure in it. I won't forget sitting next to Allan Donald at Edgbaston on the first day of the 1st Test against West Indies in June 2000 as his former captain Hansie Cronje made a live on-air match-fixing confession. Afterwards, Allan looked across at me and rather dejectedly observed: 'I wonder if my whole career is real or not.' He, like most of his team-mates, had never suspected such a thing was possible. The entire affair took everyone by surprise because cricket had not properly woken up to the fact that it was being targeted by betting scamsters. I wasn't on the 1999–2000 South Africa tour when Cronje's shenanigans occurred in the final Test, and when the initial story broke I told my editors it sounded like a load of rubbish, that Cronje was a national hero, a huge figure, and no-one should believe a word of it. Not the greatest analysis as it turned out.

No journalist ever wants to become the story but when England toured Sri Lanka in 2001 that was my lot. We'd lost the commentary rights to talkSPORT but Peter Baxter was determined that we should still do a half-hour programme every day. So he would commentate on each ball, recording it so that if anything happened he could slip in a clip during our daily round-up. In the world of broadcasting rights, it was probably a fine line and lawyers would be leaping all over it these days. TalkSPORT weren't in the slightest bit bothered but the Sri Lankan administrators decided to make a fuss. They should have simply told Peter: no commentary – you're here for news access only. Instead, they chucked us all out of the Galle International Stadium.

I had one of those early satellite phones and so we headed for Galle Fort which, although some distance away, had a brilliant view of the ground. Unfortunately there was no mains power and eventually the phone battery gave up. But I got through most of the morning schedule – Radio 5, the *Today* programme – and we were making an important point. The Sri Lankans wanted payment for news access. Once you go down that road it would have meant newspapers and photographers also paying for news access. The *Daily Mail* accused us of being pompous but how would they have felt about being charged to cover sports news? Should we have been commentating? Probably not. But it wasn't live. I said at the time that it was a sad day for cricket if the authorities were getting so greedy that they wanted to charge news outlets reporting on the game for the good of the game.

On a lighter note, I enjoyed a wonderful, panoramic view from the fort. There's a little road that runs around the back of the ground and you could watch all manner of people trundling up and down – buses, bikes and those little three-wheeled tuk-tuks. Transport for the BBC team in Sri Lanka was all by car and you kept your driver throughout the tour. Ours was a Mr Simmons, a lovely chap who did everything he could to keep the show on the road. You have a close relationship – we went to his house for dinner – and you get pretty close. Up on the fort ramparts, he decided his role was holding a coloured parasol over me for hours to keep the sun off.

ALISON

As a journalist you sometimes just happen to be in the right place at the right time. During the 2007 World Cup in the West Indies, I'd been assigned as Radio 5 Live and *TMS* reporter for Ireland v. Pakistan. It was thought this would be a routine win for Pakistan so Peter Baxter hadn't allocated a commentary team to Jamaica for the game. All of a sudden, Ireland brought themselves to the brink of pulling off a massive upset and Peter called, saying: 'We're going to have to come to you, Ali. Are you OK to commentate?' I ran down to the press box, grabbed a couple of the Ireland journalists to help, and went straight on air to bring *TMS* listeners the final overs of a brilliant Ireland win.

But, of course, that wasn't even the biggest story coming out of Jamaica. Following the result, I had to seek a reaction from Pakistan coach Bob Woolmer and that turned out to be the last interview he gave. Next morning came the awful news that he'd been discovered dead in his room at the Pegasus Hotel in Kingston and, as that filtered out, so demand from broadcasters around the world increased. Whenever I hung up on one call to a BBC radio or TV outlet there would be a load of bleeps indicating another ten voicemails had landed requesting more two-ways. Yet that was nothing compared to the frenzy which erupted a few days later when, bang in the middle of the tournament, the Director of Communications for the Jamaica Constabulary Force, Karl Angell, announced a murder investigation. At the time, the suggestion of murder was flabbergasting and dramatic but also entirely plausible given that it was coming straight from the police. Soon, various other reporters were heading to Jamaica, including a couple of BBC news stringers.

With a now insatiable demand for reports and updates, I had to be innovative with the available technology. The usual means of broadcasting live was either through a fixed-line ISDN, which was used for *TMS* commentary from Jamaica's Sabina Park, or a hefty M4 satellite dish which was heavy to lug around. To use the sat dish you had to be outdoors, in a safe zone and with a clear line of vision up to the satellite. But I didn't have an M4 because I'd not been sent to cover important breaking news – just an anticipated regulation win for Pakistan. The only way to get recordings of interviews and press conferences back from the Pegasus Hotel to BBC HQ was by feeding the audio from my mini-disc recorder down the ISDN line at Sabina Park, which was completely impractical. And my only means of broadcasting live was via my little Nokia with its dodgy phone signal.

I had a personal laptop and a reasonable grasp of technical stuff so I searched online and downloaded some audio editing software. I could now feed recordings into my PC, save them as MP3 files and email them back to the studio. But it still didn't solve the problem of going live to air until it occurred to me that if I could talk live on Skype to my family, why couldn't we use Skype for two-way interviews on the radio? I suggested this to a studio manager, who had a think, then gave me a Skype handle, and soon afterwards switched me live to a studio presenter and my voice was broadcast in almost crystal-clear sound quality. It may sound obvious now, but in 2007 no-one had tried this before at 5 Live Sport. So I still claim it as my small role in advancing broadcast technology.

AGGERS

I was with England in St Lucia at the time. I remember being told by a Jamaican former cricketer, who I won't name, that he had a good contact in the Jamaican police and that his understanding was that the Pakistan team plane taking off from Kingston would land in Montego Bay, and that two Pakistani cricketers would be immediately arrested on suspicion of murder. I actually wrote a report based on that in the back of my book, ready to go, although it was never needed as the information turned out to be completely wrong. But it does illustrate the wild rumours and guesswork that were flying around at the time. As we now know, poor Bob had probably suffered a massive heart attack, but the court recorded an open verdict.

I was working on a TV highlights show which would normally have gone out live. However, a live show would have been too late for our guest, the England opening batsman Ed Joyce, so we'd recorded it an hour in advance and it was already being edited in London when Alison called to say that Bob had died. That was obviously a hammer-blow for all of us who knew him. I was very fond of him and had spent a lot of time with Bob over the years and often seemed to get him out. We used to joke that if I bowled him an orange he'd smack it straight to square leg and get caught. Over dinner, he'd sometimes explain his on-field tactics by moving the salt and pepper pots around. He was great company. So the shock of him dying was terrible but to hear he might have been murdered was unthinkable.

There was now also a practical problem for the BBC team. Our recorded preview had finished with the England opening bat Ed Joyce swinging on the end of a pirate rope amid much hilarity and comments on the lines of England players swinging into their next game. But as soon as Alison broke the news I realised it couldn't possibly be broadcast. I phoned our editor in London to explain it had to be pulled – his immediate reaction was, well, it's going out in ten minutes. There was no alternative but to junk the recording and do the whole half-hour show live and unscripted with myself and co-presenter Manish Bhasin doing a tribute to Bob. Alison contributed on the phone and together we tried to bring viewers up to speed with this extraordinary news coming out of Kingston, Jamaica.

ALISON

The following year we again found ourselves at the centre of another enormous news story – this time the terrible loss of life caused by the Mumbai terror attacks. My role on that tour had been to give Radio 5 Live updates. We'd checked out of the Taj Mahal Palace hotel a few days before it all happened and headed off for the one-dayers. I remember us driving back from Cuttack, eastern India, in semi-darkness and our assistant producer Shilpa Patel getting a text message asking if we were OK, and then something about a bomb. Once we reached our hotel in Cuttack, the full horror became clear. We'd been due to check back into the Taj Mahal for the Test series but everyone, the England team included, was flown home and there was a lot of uncertainty about whether the tour would resume. We all got called to a meeting in the basement of Television Centre, Wood Lane, London, to be asked if we'd be prepared to return to India if England returned. We agreed that we would, and the tour was reassigned to venues at Chennai and Mohali, which were seen as safer and easier to police.

The Chennai match was memorable not just because of the extraordinary level of security but because the media was making quite a thing out of the fact that Sachin Tendulkar didn't often score big, match-winning, second-innings hundreds for India. England had seemed well on top in Chennai, and set India a record run chase, but on the penultimate evening of the game Virender Sehwag opened the batting and pilloried the England attack. Then Tendulkar took control. The following day, he moved effortlessly through the gears before unfurling a four to both give him that elusive 100 and win the match for India. He dedicated his century to the people of Mumbai – he's from that city himself – and it is one of the most moving cricketing moments I've ever experienced. It was as though his innings had a wider healing power for the people of India. Only the cricketing god that was Sachin Tendulkar could have had that impact.

AGGERS

Everyone at *TMS* gets sent on a hostile environment course because we do operate in some fairly interesting parts of the world. Simply being a stranger stuck in a big crowd can leave you vulnerable and we had one tricky moment in Chittagong during the 2011 World Cup when Bangladesh beat England in a thrilling group game. We ended up outside the ground amid huge numbers of people packed together in the streets and no obvious way to extricate ourselves.

Of course, sometimes it's the authorities you must be wary of. During the last *TMS* tour to South Africa in 2019–20 I was driving Michael Vaughan, Henry Blofeld and Simon Mann when we were pulled over by an armed policeman. I particularly don't like the road between Johannesburg and Centurion, a half-hour drive, because at certain points you do feel vulnerable. This officer demanded to see my driving licence, which was back at the hotel. He got very aggressive and forced me down on the car bonnet, at which point Michael Vaughan helpfully tweeted a photo of me with the caption: 'It's not looking good for Aggers here.' It all got very heated and the policeman insisted on me paying a fine; he just wanted money. So we had a whipround. Blowers contributed nothing, Simon and I had a few rand and Michael had only a £10 note. This all got handed over and fortunately it was enough to let us get away.

WRONG LINE

The Allen Stanford affair

For sheer national sporting embarrassment, the Stanford affair takes some beating. In essence, the US businessman Allen Stanford, later a convicted fraudster, took advantage of the England and Wales Cricket Board's fear that their best players would be lured by the newly formed Indian Premier League – reducing availability for England duty. In June 2008, Stanford, who seemed to be dripping in dollars earned through his Antigua-based bank, cut a $100 million deal with the ECB for five T20 games between England and his West Indies 'Stanford Superstars XI'. The winners of the first game would receive $20 million – about £12 million at the time – with $1 million going to each player, $1 million split between whichever four members of the winning squad didn't make the XI, $1 million split between the winning management team and the remaining $7 million divvied up between the England and West Indies cricket boards. The losing team would not get a cent.

As an exercise in dividing players into the haves and the have-nots, it could hardly have been better conceived. In England's case, members of the Test team who had served their country magnificently – including captain Michael Vaughan, James Anderson and the ever-reliable Alastair Cook – would not get a look-in because they were not T20 specialists. Attempts by the ECB to present the entire circus as some kind of good cause to benefit

West Indies cricket were risible. As for England coach Peter Moores citing the pride of playing for the England badge, Cook had an answer to that. The match, he pointed out, was meaningless to players without the cheques at the end of it. Yet none of this mattered to Allen Stanford as he landed at Lord's in a swish black helicopter, waving at non-existent friends for the TV cameras, hugging ECB chairman Giles Clarke and flaunting a Perspex suitcase supposedly containing his $20 million.

England went on to play, and lose, against the Stanford Superstars in Antigua in November. The game was irrelevant to most cricket fans but the PR surrounding it was toe-curlingly embarrassing for the ECB as photos emerged of the Texas tycoon bouncing the wife of an England player on his knee as other wives and partners clustered around. Within nine months, the whole farcical charade had collapsed. It emerged that the FBI had launched a fraud investigation into Stanford's business empire and in February 2009 the ECB cancelled all contracts with him. Stanford's wealth was an illusion, an elaborate Ponzi-style scam in which money from new savers and investors was used to finance returns to existing ones. Barely $200,000 of the $7 billion Stanford accumulated was recovered, he was found guilty on 13 specimen fraud charges and in 2012 a Houston judge sentenced him to 110 years in prison.

AGGERS

You try never to get personally too involved in any story but when you love cricket and see it being used and manipulated for nefarious purposes it's hard not to feel outrage. So when the US businessman Allen Stanford landed by helicopter at Lord's in 2008, a suitcase supposedly stuffed with dollars at his side, it made me want to vomit. All the cricket writers were furious – not because of him, we didn't know anything about him – but for English cricket to cut this deal, to throw a hand grenade into team spirit, to make players compete in a ludicrous winner-takes-all game in Antigua for a million dollars apiece; it was just utterly vulgar and not what the sport was about. Yes, the administrators were under pressure because they did somehow have to try and stop their best players being lured out to the Indian Premier League. But Stanford was not the right partner and not the way to counter any potential exodus. The entire enterprise was always going to end in tears because it was so divisive and hadn't been thought through on any front or on any level. The reality only dawned on the players when they actually turned up for Stanford's ludicrous tournament in November 2008. Without doubt it was an ugly blot on the landscape of English cricket and the only time I've ever known England supporters pleased that their team lost. We discussed it all on *TMS* and I made very clear why I thought it was wrong. It was ripping the team apart.

TUFFERS

Touching down in his chopper with a suitcase supposedly full of cash did seem rather a rum do for the Home of Cricket. But I'm not a journalist, I didn't know his background and I initially took his involvement at face value. Here was Stanford's money coming into the game – great for players, helping lift cricket's profile – and at first glance it was an all-round win. I received £1500 for my last Test match, that's £300 per day, minus tax, and minus a fine I got for something or other, so my generation of cricketers weren't big earners. I have no problem with that because the game has been wonderful to me. But times change. When Stanford turned up you can understand why he got players' attention.

And yet, among the *TMS* team, there was a growing feeling that Stanford didn't 'get' cricket and, worse, that something about his sponsorship offer was shifty. As we now know, shifty was an understatement. In fact, some of those who took the Stanford dollar were persuaded by him to reinvest with his bank and, surprise, surprise, they ended up with sod all.

The year after Stanford's fraud was exposed we saw another example of cricket being manipulated by cunning criminals. I was doing a *TMS* summariser stint for the England v. Pakistan 4th Test at Lord's in 2010, the game now notorious for the 'no-ball betting scam'. At the moment it happened none of us had a clue anything shifty was going on, although, as the TV replays appeared, Aggers just turned to me and said something like: 'That's a huge no-ball,' meaning the bowler had way overstepped the delivery crease. A couple of days later, as the truth began to unfold, we came into work feeling shocked and even a bit stupid. The commentary box had a sad atmosphere as though a piece of our beloved sport had been taken away. We felt cheated about what we were watching. Were these games really competitive or were elements pre-ordained? Were people sacrificing their wicket for a duck in exchange for a bung? And how could we really put energy into talking about something that might turn out to be a load of old bollocks? I even started thinking about my own career, although nobody ever seemed to get out for nought when I was bowling. They were more likely to post 100-plus.

AGGERS

Aside from the anger about corruption tainting cricket, I felt most sorry for Stuart Broad. He went on to score a brilliant 169 in that match but because three Pakistan players were conspiring to produce deliberate no-balls to order, a cloud of suspicion still hangs over that game. It's unfair because the no-balls were irrelevant to Stuart's innings. Corruption exists in all sport and my view is that every time someone gets caught the punishment should make it harder for the next person to try. If people can't believe what they are seeing, and are still having to pay to watch, then all integrity is gone and the sport is finished.

WRONG LINE
The no-ball spot-fixing scam

The exponential growth of gambling via smartphones and websites has left many sports vulnerable to spot-fixing – the practice by which a corrupt player seeks to influence a specific part of a match rather than the match itself. Which is exactly what Pakistan bowlers Mohammad Amir and Mohammad Asif, with the connivance of their captain Salman Butt, attempted to do on the morning of the 4th Test against England at Lord's on 26 August 2010. Unfortunately for them, the entire scam had been penetrated by the *News of the World* newspaper and the evidence it published three days later was damning. Undercover reporters had met sports agent Mazhar Majeed who, they believed, was implicated in match-fixing for a betting ring. Majeed took a £140,000 fixer's fee from the journalists – not realising he had received marked notes – and told them that the first ball of Amir's third over would be a no-ball and the sixth delivery of the tenth over, from Mohammad Asif, would be another. Butt's involvement was necessary because otherwise Majeed could not guarantee that the two fast bowlers would be in action when required. The entire conversation was recorded by the *News of the World* and both Amir, only 18 at the time, and Asif overstepped the crease in their delivery strides precisely as Majeed had promised.

When the story broke, the three players immediately maintained their innocence. They were backed in the UK by the High

Commissioner for Pakistan, who claimed they had been 'set up' and were innocent of any crime. However, Scotland Yard immediately launched a fraud inquiry and all three were quickly suspended by the ICC. They received lengthy cricket bans of between five and ten years but that proved the least of their problems. They and Majeed were charged with cheating at gambling and receiving corrupt payments, and in November 2011 were handed down prison sentences at Southwark Crown Court ranging from six months to two years and eight months. In a press statement outside court, Crown Prosecution Service barrister Sally Walsh said: 'People who had paid good money to see a professional and exciting game of cricket on the famous ground at Lord's had no idea that what they were watching was not a true game but one where part of the game had been pre-determined for cash. Butt and Asif denied any wrong-doing but the jury has decided after hearing all the evidence that what happened on the crease that day was criminal in the true sense of the word.'

TOP LIST

Best fast bowlers faced or watched

AGGERS On his day, at Lord's in 1972, Australia's Bob Massie. Swung the ball massively.

TUFFERS Wasim Akram and Waqar Younis, swinging the ball around corners, and Malcolm Marshall, who was skiddy, quick and had a great bouncer, are all right up there for me. Then there's Allan Donald, Shaun Pollock, Patrick Patterson, Merv Hughes, Courtney Walsh, Curtly Ambrose – the list is endless and they all bloody well terrified me. Anything over 70 mph terrified me. And even if you weren't that fast but ran in looking scary, that was terrifying enough. If I had to choose one, though, it would be Waqar. Until he arrived no-one had heard of reverse swing. The batters were told to see off the risks of the new ball and then things would get easier. But Waqar, particularly, turned that on its head. There were times against Pakistan when we'd slump from around 100 for 1 to 180 all out. You'd ask yourselves; how did that happen with an old ball? But Waqar would be bowling at 80 mph-plus and swinging the ball in a foot to hit your toes.

ISA The best bowler I faced was Australia's Cathryn Fitzpatrick. She was something of a legend so being able to navigate her as a young player in 2005 when she was still bowling late-70s mph was very satisfying. Among bowlers I have watched, Dale Steyn at his best was incredible. He had the pace, the swing, the ability to intimidate. It was so sad that his career was cut short by a string of injuries.

EBONY Cathryn Fitzpatrick. In my early days, I had the audacity to try a couple of shots against her. She was not impressed. In women's cricket, the bowling speeds tend to be slower, so you play on the front foot. That didn't work against Cathryn and I was fending balls off my collarbone. I watched her for years as a kid growing up and to play against the greatest female bowler of my lifetime to date was amazing. Among fast bowlers generally, then Curtly Ambrose and Courtney Walsh. I grew up watching them. It wasn't just that they were fast and lethal – they were metronomic in accuracy.

CARLOS The hardest I had to cope with was Sri Lanka's Lasith Malinga, aptly known as 'The Slinger'. It was difficult to pick up the ball's flight from his low delivery angle. I used to have a similar problem with the West Indies' Fidel Edwards.

ALISON Curtly Ambrose. I had a huge affinity with him anyway because he was Northamptonshire's overseas player for many years and it felt like he was ours. He petrified batters – especially Tuffers – and I'm not surprised. His snarl, the flash of that wristband as he cocked his wrist before delivering a rocket – it must have been a truly unwelcome sight. Love him as I did, it was hard to watch him dismantling England.

AATIF In terms of wicket-taking I can't separate Wasim Akram and Waqar Younis. But in terms of being *actually* deadly, then Shoaib Akhtar. Facing him, my focus would be entirely on staying alive. I will never forget his cut-throat gesture to fellow fast bowler Brett Lee.

CHAPTER 12

SPOOFS, BLUNDERS AND WIND-UPS

In which Aggers and Tuffers revisit some classic commentary-box comedy – intentional and otherwise.

AGGERS

Spoofs have always been a trademark of *TMS* and the period between 1991, when I arrived, and 1994, when Johnners retired, was what you might call our golden years. I take a large share of the responsibility. It was impossible to understate the joy of catching out Brian or Blowers on air and when Geoffrey Boycott joined us he proved another heaven-sent pranking victim. It must also be said that I suffered too, including one particularly sophisticated set-up by Johnners in which I was conned into believing I was doing a live interview on the BBC's Saturday afternoon sports show *Grandstand*. Brian engaged half a BBC Outside Broadcast unit to pull that one off.

Bill Frindall took on responsibility for vetting the letters we received because he regarded himself as an expert at spotting spoofs submitted by the rest of us. But, like all the older members of the *TMS* team, he was not good on technology. None of them had any idea how computers worked and fax machines were a mystery. To them, it was all rocket science. So for a few years we spoofers were in our pomp. I could sit behind Johnners in the commentary box, with a fairly basic laptop, create a realistic-looking business letterhead and then send it in as a fax. It gave me enormous satisfaction to see it instantly emerging from the *TMS* fax machine and handed over to Brian. Eventually Peter Baxter got wise to my tactics and would regularly go across to check faxes. The art was to rip spoofs off the machine before he knew they were there and then plant them right in front of Johnners or Blowers, who would dutifully read them out.

Blowers liked to plug things. He once cut a deal with Air New Zealand and for a while every other plane zooming over a Test ground was faithfully described to listeners as an incoming service from some far-flung corner of New Zealand. He had to be nabbed so I sent him a fax from a fake carpet company called Stephenson's of Sheffield who promised him a free carpet if he gave them a mention on air. Blowers willingly obliged, warbling on about what a marvellous job Stephenson's were doing and what marvellous carpets they sold. He then carefully folded up the fax and popped it in his breast pocket so that he knew the name of the contact who would be providing his free carpet. But then the next fax, which had already been prepared, was fired in from Jones's Carpets of Sheffield, complaining about how outrageous it was that their main competitor had been given free advertising and that they would be reporting Blowers to the BBC's director general unless their name also featured in the programme. So he then had to go on about how Sheffield was packed full of excellent carpet shops, including his old friends at Jones's Carpets. He then hurriedly pulled out the Stephenson's letter and chucked it in a bin.

The art of a good spoof was always to ensure your target had no time to read things in advance. At Edgbaston, Johnners was once assigned to describe the presentation of players to senior executives from Cornhill Insurance, the company sponsoring the match. Sponsors always provided us with a list of VIPs but on this occasion Johnners couldn't find it. That's because I'd squirrelled it away to carefully Tipp-Ex out the name of Cornhill's general manager Cecil Burrows, type in a replacement and photocopy the doctored version. As Johnners frantically scrabbled through his papers I produced the list with a flourish and slapped it down in front of him.

With a grateful nod, Johnners grabbed it and began: 'Down there on the podium we have A. C. Smith, secretary of the Test and County Cricket Board, the man-of-the-match adjudicator Fred Trueman and the general manager of Cornhill Insurance, Hugh Jarce.' He carried on, oblivious to his colleagues collapsing helplessly behind him.

Faking documents became our stock-in-trade for a while. When preparing to interview a 'View from the Boundary' guest, you had to call up their newspaper cuttings from the BBC library. That really was an open goal. You simply mocked up a fake biography, peppered it with completely false, though believable, nuggets of personal information and popped it into an envelope labelled 'additional information from the BBC' along with a fake researcher ID. During the nineties, BBC Radio was busily reallocating programmes across the network and it was decided we would move over to Radio 3 medium wave to share Radio 3 FM airtime with that station's classical music output. So in order to placate Radio 3 listeners, who were rather more keen on Bach and Beethoven than ball-by-ball commentary, Peter Baxter asked the acclaimed orchestral conductor James Judd to come on.

David 'Bumble' Lloyd was doing a stint with us at the time and we immediately got to work. Rightly suspecting that Johnners wouldn't have a clue who James Judd was, we smuggled into his cuttings file a

typewritten profile in which it was revealed that James kept ferrets
for a hobby and as a result had been nicknamed Ratty by his
musicians. He arrived at the commentary box to be jovially greeted
by Johnners, 'Ah, Ratty, do come on in,' which must have been
bewildering for our guest. But James politely said nothing and kept a
straight face for much of the interview in which he was questioned
on his work with the Reykjavik Philharmonic, his love of
Wimbledon FC (or some such team) and a stream of other entirely
spurious personal claims. We were rumbled in the end but
fortunately James had a sense of humour. He later sent us all box
sets of his latest CD, signed 'with best wishes, Ratty'.

After that, there was no stopping us. When the former England
batsman Graeme Fowler did a season as a *TMS* summariser he was
handed the job of interviewing his boyhood hero, the Manchester
United and England footballer Nobby Stiles. On the appointed
morning, Graeme proudly told us on air how he'd got some great
additional information from the library and did we know that
Nobby used to do freefall parachute jumping for charity. Nobby
was driving to the ground when he heard this and almost drove into
a tree.

The parachute wind-up was later dusted down and presented to
another *TMS* colleague, Jeremy Coney, who had a 15-minute live
sports slot on a New Zealand TV station. Jeremy asked me for a few
stories about his guest, the former fast bowler John Snow, and was
informed that John had raised hundreds of thousands of pounds
for charities through his freefall parachuting hobby. When Jeremy
brought this up halfway through their interview, the camera cut to

Snowy who looked nonplussed and pointed out he'd never been near a parachute. Then the likely truth dawned. 'Jeremy,' he replied gently, 'have you been talking to Aggers?'

Perhaps this kind of thing wouldn't happen these days but we're supposed to be in the entertainment business and the listeners loved it. Maybe this is why Peter Baxter tolerated our japes. But he did worry that things might get out of hand and that Johnners or Blowers, the more vulnerable among us, would unintentionally read out something too edgy for the BBC. Of all things, it was a version of the Shipping Forecast which almost evaded Peter's defences.

For several years on Radio 4, we had to go over to the Shipping Forecast at midday. It became an iconic element of the programme and listeners seemed to enjoy it, provided they didn't miss any action. One day, our continuity announcer Andrew Crawford, obviously bored, produced a *TMS* version which was cleverly crafted to conceal a verbal hand grenade. He faxed it over to us at the Oval and I showed it to Blowers, pointing out Andrew's tweaks – for instance 'North Utsire' had become 'North of Shilpa', a reference to our assistant producer Shilpa Patel. But I'd carefully kept my thumb over Andrew's version of Rockall. Blowers thought it was marvellous and gamely began reading the renamed sea areas to our audience. However, Peter must have noticed a sense of anticipation in the commentary box and was suspicious. Suddenly, he saw what was coming, dived dramatically across the box like a slip going for a catch and snatched the sheet from Blowers's grasp just as Henry was about to get to F**kall. It was The Spoof That Got Away.

In 1993, I stitched Johnners up with a fake *TMS* live broadcast and I should have known he would get his own back. I'd done something on women's cricket for BBC Saturday sports show *Grandstand* and the following week the producer Keith Mackenzie came into the *TMS* box saying it was a really nice piece and could they use me later for a live *Grandstand* interview on why England can't find fast bowlers. I thought, 'OK, here's a career opportunity,' Peter Baxter seemed fine with it so at tea I climbed up all this scaffolding to the TV studio at Edgbaston.

Soon the floor manager Steve Pearson is powdering me and wiring up this huge earpiece and there's Jack Bannister and Fred Trueman waiting to be interviewed. Fred has his shirt hanging out and is smoking a massive cigar, I've got Keith in my ear, the whole crew is on standby, and off we go. But when I put my first question to Jack – why was it that England couldn't produce fast bowlers? – he replied: 'I dunno.' And that was it. Fred said nothing either and I soon started sweating. All I could hear was Keith going mad, shouting louder and louder. Then Fred started burbling on about damp-proof courses and salmon fishing. None of this felt right, and you can spot my shifty glances around the studio. Yet I had to plough on. Only when I heard a voice in my ear saying, 'I think the long-nosed commentator [i.e. Johnners] has got his revenge,' did it all become clear. I guess it would never happen today.

Geoffrey Boycott worked with us as a summariser for many years and his favourite phrases would crop up most days. You could download a Boycott Bingo card off the internet which listed them – observations such as: 'I've seen more brains in a pork pie'; 'listen, I played for Yorkshire'; 'powder puff bowling'; 'the corridor of uncertainty' and 'I could have hit that with a stick of rooooobarb'. Geoffrey didn't realise there were people at home ticking these phrases off on their card, including the former UK Prime Minister David Cameron. So, during one soporific Test at the Oval, England v. Pakistan, we tried to steer him right through the card in a single day. For the most part he didn't need any prompting but the one phrase he hadn't produced was his standard disdainful opinion of a dropped catch: 'My mum could have caught that in her pinny.'

As we neared the end of play it seemed this one would elude us. But then Mohammad Yousuf obligingly missed a sitter in the covers, and I seized the moment by suggesting Geoffrey's mum would have pouched it. He agreed but at first offered only that it was 'pretty straightforward'. I persisted: 'Come on, Geoffrey, that's a bit tame. We all know what you're thinking.' And, eventually, out it came: 'Yeah, all right, my mum could have caught that in her pinny.' And from the back of the commentary box up went the triumphant cry: 'House!'

My favourite bit of Boycott-baiting was a wind-up devised by our *TMS* statistician, Andrew Samson. In July 2017, I got to the Oval early for the final day of England's game against South Africa to hear Geoffrey banging on about the fortieth anniversary of his one hundredth first-class century scored at his beloved Headingley. I said to Andrew: 'Is he driving you mad too?' It was agreed we had to get something organised and, within a very short space of time, Andrew had the idea of cancelling out his hundredth hundred. This was exactly the right button to press. I knew about Geoffrey's 'hundred hundreds' anniversary dinner because he'd invited me to attend. Suddenly everything clicked into place. I wrote a spoof press release from the ICC stating that all statistics relating to the 1970 England v. Rest of the World series would be downgraded, in other words the five games would no longer have first-class status. Geoffrey had scored 157 in the fifth of those and so of course his dinner would actually be celebrating the anniversary of his ninety-ninth first-class hundred.

The reason, the press statement claimed, was because the South African government felt the series had amounted to political interference. It had replaced a planned South Africa tour to England and involved several Springboks, including Mike Proctor and Barry Richards, at a time when South Africa should have been isolated from international sport over apartheid. So there was a sense of plausibility about the thing. Henry Moeran performed some technological wizardry on the header page to make it look genuine and I then started preparing the groundwork in commentary. Geoffrey was summarising alongside me and fortunately nothing much happened in the cricket as England cruised to a win.

I mentioned that we'd been alerted to a major announcement from the ICC, which would be coming through soon. A few minutes later, Henry brought over my press release and I began by saying: 'Oh, this isn't what we were expecting.' And I started reading it. Andrew then chipped in, asking Geoffrey: 'You got a century in that series, didn't you? There'll be a bit of a problem if that is taken out.' I became conscious of Geoffrey leaning further and further over my shoulder reading the 'quotes from an ICC spokesperson'. After a few seconds he exploded: 'Isn't it ridiculous? Write to him, he's an idiot . . . there might be others who got a hundred and other records.' The whole episode went on for about ten minutes until Geoffrey fumed: 'It's a mess, isn't it? A complete mess.' To which I replied: 'It's also a complete wind-up' and screwed up the press release. Geoffrey delivered his standard rebuke – 'You muppet' – followed by 'It's never . . . is that a wind-up? You muppet, Agnew, I'll get you for that.' In fairness he took it well and even obtained a video recording to play at his dinner. After it was over, I got a congratulatory phone call from Peter Hain, one of our former 'View from the Boundary' guests and a leading campaigner against apartheid.

NICE LINE

Boycott's innings

Sir Geoffrey Boycott OBE ranks among England's finest opening bats with over 8000 Test runs to his name. His average of 47.72 runs accumulated over 108 Tests is world class by any measure and in only 20 of those matches did he end up on the losing side. The former *TMS* commentator John Arlott once observed that 'any expectation of an English win, except in freak bowling conditions, is based on a major innings from Boycott'.

Boycott announced his retirement from *TMS* in 2020 after 14 years as a summariser. On social media he wrote: 'I have thoroughly enjoyed it and just love cricket with a passion. I also wish to thank all those that have said how much they have enjoyed my commentary and for those that haven't – too bad.' The former Yorkshire batter could also not resist a playful sign-off aimed at his friend and spoofer-in-chief, Aggers. 'Hopefully,' he added, 'I may still have some input . . . if that tall, lanky ex-Leicestershire medium-pace bowler needs an honest appraisal or wants to take the mickey out of me maybe he will give me a call while on air.'

I began my *TMS* career as a summariser during England's 1991 home Test series against the West Indies, the idea being that I would find my feet before pitching in as a commentator myself later that year. It was soon obvious that, during a break in play, Brian Johnston loved nothing better than reading out, and commenting on, listeners' letters. So it was that I found myself sitting next to him as he read out one from a Mr Ian Richter in Baghdad. 'He says he loves listening to the cricket commentary because it keeps him in touch with home,' chortled Johnners, seemingly oblivious to the fact that the first Gulf War had ended only months earlier. 'Yes, lovely in Baghdad this time of year, marvellous, lots of flowers, plenty of sun. Thank you, Mr Richter, and I'm sure you'll be enjoying a nice cocktail later.'

The problem, of course, was that Mr Richter was actually in prison in Baghdad on some trumped-up spying charge and his only luxury was a little short-wave radio. In fairness to Johnners the letter didn't mention that he was banged up – I guess he couldn't write that – but Johnners was horrified when he found out the next day and apologised on air. In fact, Ian was released that winter and later came on 'View from the Boundary' to give us the full story. In prison, he'd somehow got hold of the BBC World Service magazine *London Calling*, which provided listings for short-wave programmes, and realised he could tune in to the *TMS* World Service feed. He also confirmed he'd heard Johnners's apology. He told us: 'For the first three years I was in solitary, so I had virtually nothing. But eventually I got a radio and I started playing with it. And I managed to get a copy of *London Calling*, which announced they were having a ball-by-ball service and I tuned in quite fruitlessly one morning. I then, quite by chance, discovered that if I listened to a certain frequency, once it had finished shortly after UK lunchtime, if I twiddled the knob a little further to the left, I would pick up the southeastern wavelength where it was being beamed to. It was rather faint, but if I cocked an ear to one side and told everyone to shut up – I was rather fierce about that – I would have four or five hours' cricket. So it was wonderful.'

Arguably the most famous *TMS* clip of all was 'The Legover', not so much a blunder by Johnners as a stitch-up by me. It was the second day of the 5th Test, August 1991, England v. West Indies at the Oval. England played really well in this game and eventually won by 5 wickets to draw the series 2–2. However, for *TMS* fans the only memory of the match that mattered was the moment Ian Botham got himself out 'hit wicket'. England had batted first and were in a strong position when Botham stepped back too far to a short-pitched ball from Curtly Ambrose, tried to hop over the stumps, failed and knocked off a bail. Later, the players came off for bad light and it fell to Johnners and me to do a summary of the day's play. When we got to the Botham incident, Johnners was as usual wading into dangerous waters, referring to Botham's 'inner thigh', but when I replied that 'he didn't quite get his legover' it wasn't even an original line. I'd borrowed it from the *Sun's* cricket writer John Etheridge who a little earlier had predicted his newspaper's back-page headline would be: 'Botham cocks it up by not getting his legover'.

It has never been properly documented but Bill Frindall played a key role in the 45 seconds which followed. The whole business would never have lasted so long had it not been for one of his impromptu snorts. Until that point, Brian was recovering composure but the snort sent him over the edge and there was no way of clawing himself back. If you listen carefully to the recording, you hear two crucial things. As I observe that Botham 'didn't quite get his legover' – there's a loud chink of china, which is Bill at the back of the commentary box slamming his cup of tea down on to its saucer in a gesture encompassing both horror and delight at what would surely come. Johnners carries on gamely, trying to stifle his giggles, and even manages to mention David Lawrence's brief cameo innings. But just as he mentions Lawrence you hear the Frindall Snort. And that was it. Brian was gone. This is now the most familiar clip of his entire broadcasting career. However, another cameo attributed to him, by him, supposedly during another England v. West Indies game when Michael Holding was bowling to Peter Willey, is an urban myth. It was claimed that Brian had said on air: 'The bowler's Holding, the batsman's Willey.' I'm sure he would have loved to have said it and perhaps he did in some theatre talk. But on *TMS*, at least, it never happened.

NICE LINE
'The Legover' commentary

Johnners: Botham – out in the most extraordinary way.

Aggers: Oh, it was ever so sad really. It was interesting because he'd just started to loosen up and look for those big blows through the off side, anything a little bit wide. I remember saying it looks as though Ian Botham is starting to play his own way. It was a bouncer and he tried to hook it – why he tried to hook Ambrose I'm not sure because on this sort of pitch it's a very difficult prospect – it smacked him on the helmet, I think.

Johnners: Shoulder, I think.

Aggers: Shoulder, was it? Well, he tried to hook and he lost his balance and he knew – this is the tragic thing about it – he knew exactly what was going to happen, he tried to step over the stumps and just flicked a bail with his right leg.

Johnners: He tried to do the splits over it and the inner part of his thigh must have just removed the bails.

Aggers: He couldn't quite get his legover.

For a while Johnners carries on gamely, although keen-eared listeners must have noted the genesis of a giggle.

Johnners: Anyhow, he did very well indeed, batting 131 minutes and hit three fours and then we had Lewis playing extremely well for his 47 not out ... Aggers, do stop it. And he was joined by DeFreitas who was in for 40 minutes, a useful little partnership there, they put on 35 in 40 minutes before he was caught by Dujon off Walsh. Lawrence, always entertaining, batted for thirty ... thirty-five ... thirt ... thirty-five minutes ... hit a four over the wicketkeeper's ... Aggers, for goodness sake, stop it ...

Aggers (supposedly to the rescue): Yes, Lawrence, 'stremely well ...

Johnners eventually regained control but went home convinced he was in for a rocket from *TMS* producer Peter Baxter and possibly even the sack. Fortunately, listeners came to the rescue with hundreds of phone calls and letters saying it was the funniest thing they'd ever heard on radio.

Despite us getting away with 'The Legover', Peter Baxter decided it would be better to keep Johnners and me apart for a while. He had to reunite us eventually, though, because people kept writing in asking whether we'd been separated in class for being troublesome. The following year, he tried us out for a *TMS* letters session during a break at Old Trafford, which should have been straightforward but turned into another nightmare. Bizarrely, and I never understood why this should be, we never got a chance to read the letters first. Instead, Peter would stand behind us, opening them and placing each one in front of us alternately. And he kicked off with what amounted to a hospital pass in rugby terms. It was from a William H. Titt and as soon as I saw the name I knew I couldn't say it out loud. It was all about the review procedure; why was it even necessary? If the umpire said a batsman was out then he *was* out. I went as cold as a corpse – why was this happening to us again – and I somehow burbled: 'It's from Berkshire.'

Johnners said, 'Oh, give it here,' which was absolutely fatal. He looked at the name and instantly began struggling. All he could think to say was: 'Well, it's not the Prime Minister William Pitt, this is from William H. Titt.' And then he collapsed. He tried so hard to stifle his giggles and even went completely silent for a few seconds, thinking he might get away with it. I was laughing so Fred Trueman or somebody filled the void, saying the umpires were coming out. Johnners by now was making strange weeping noises and had to be led to the back of the commentary box. Later, he wrote to Mr Titt apologising for laughing at his name. He never got a reply, although I believe the gentleman did write in again a few years later. I'm sure it was a genuine letter because Peter was by then extremely good at spotting and rejecting spoofs and he'd handed this one to us.

Of all our summarisers, Trevor Bailey was arguably the most concise in his assessments. Admirable that may have been but it wasn't much help when, as commentator, you had to fill out the final minute or so of a *TMS* programme. On one occasion in 1993, England were in Chennai getting thoroughly thumped during the 2nd Test of their India tour. Trevor had missed the 1st Test and so, to wind things up, I thought it would be a nice idea to ask his thoughts on the three Indian spinners – Venkatapathy Raju, Anil Kumble and Rajesh Chauhan – who he was seeing for the first time. I helpfully handed him this trio's bowling figures, set out in Bill Frindall's immaculate handwriting, but unfortunately Trevor had mislaid his glasses and could barely read a thing. Somewhat agitated, but determined to plough on, he declared in magisterial style: 'Kimble? Good bowler. Ragi? Ordinary. Shoosson? Chucker.' In eight words he managed to incorrectly pronounce two of the bowlers' names while denigrating them, while simultaneously juggling the surname of India batsman Vinod Kambli with that of Anil Kumble. It was a shocker of a summary. All I could say was: 'Well thanks, Trevor, for your insight. Goodbye everyone.' And thankfully the music fired up.

Innuendo has always been a *TMS* speciality. However, as a commentator you have to make it sound as though you never meant to say anything risqué. In 1992, Eleanor Oldroyd and I were in a studio at Lord's doing a scene-setter before the start of play. She kicked off with: 'The good news is that Ian Botham's groin is back to full strength.' She instantly realised what she'd said and her face turned puce. I tried to answer that but the whole thing broke down into mini-hysterics. I mean, what can you do?

Innuendo also impinges on the names of cricketers. Tuffers was on for *TMS* when the new Pakistan opener Fakhar Zaman came to the wicket during the 2017 ICC Champions Trophy final against India. As soon as we saw his name on the team sheet we thought, 'Well, this could be tricky.' Now, you have to remember that on *TMS* we are very often trying to stitch up the person sitting next to us, be that a summariser or a new commentator taking over. I am particularly guilty but others do it too and in his day Johnners was a state-of-the-art stitcher-upper. Sometimes the listeners get it and sometimes they don't.

Anyway, I quickly clock that Fakhar is opening the batting. I can feel Johnners looking down at me from above and so I decide that throughout his innings I would refer to him only as Zaman. Once he was out, however, there would be a couple of Fakhars thrown into the commentary and then he'd be gone and we could all move on. But then the Decision Review System provided the perfect opportunity to stitch up a summariser. Who just happened to be Tuffers.

I'm commentating when, with Pakistan on 8, Zaman flashes outside the off stump and is caught behind. There's a big roar from the India supporters but then everyone realises he's not walking back to the pavilion. I tell the listeners that Fakhar's hanging about, that he doesn't want to go and that the umpires are reviewing a possible no-ball. Then I say: 'Fakhar's had a reprieve, he will come back, it's a no-ball and a free hit as well. What a lucky . . . chap.' That completely did for Tuffers.

Over the years, there are a few old chestnuts I like to throw at Phil when we're on air. I live in the Vale of Belvoir (pronounced 'beaver'), which includes parts of Leicestershire, Nottinghamshire and Lincolnshire. I mention the Belvoir a lot when we're on together – comments like, 'It was damp in the Belvoir this morning, Tuffers,' usually render him helpless. However, my favourite deployment came when we had the chef Tommy Banks on 'View from the Boundary' and he was explaining how to forage for food. At the end, I brought Tuffers into the conversation and asked: 'Did you hear that, Tuffers? I can't wait to go foraging in the Belvoir tonight.' He and I have a lot of fun. He's my main sidekick.

TUFFERS

You have to accept that Aggers has good timing. When he switched to me after that lucky Fakhar comment our listeners heard only silence. And that was because I was under the table trying to bite something to conceal my laughter. The first time he did the Belvoir on me was at the Oval, completely without warning. He and I were kicking off *TMS* and he started with a few pleasantries. How was my drive in? Fine, thanks. Any rain around? No, nothing at all. Then suddenly from nowhere he said: 'Well, it was a bit damp in the Belvoir this morning.' I had no inkling that he was referring to the Vale of Belvoir nor that Belvoir was pronounced 'beaver'. For an agonisingly long time, I was unable to speak. He still loves dropping that phrase in to take me off guard.

Aggers doesn't always mean to seize on an innuendo but if the commentary takes him down a certain road he just can't resist it. In June 2011, he was commentating on the 2nd Test between England and Sri Lanka at Lord's when Kevin Pietersen had to pause his innings so that the split rubber on his bat handle could be replaced. 'It's not easy to do that,' said Aggers. 'You've got to roll it on down the stick and make sure it is all in place with no floppy stuff on the end . . . you can't have that.' When the problem arose with Pietersen's bat handle Aggers immediately spotted it – then realised he'd referred on air to a broken rubber. It wasn't intentional but once it was done he ran with the double-meaning mercilessly, during which time everyone in the box was convulsing in group hysterics. It would have been difficult for anyone to criticise Aggers' comments because they absolutely did apply to the difficulty of putting on a new bat-handle rubber. But listeners love an innuendo and they all knew what was happening. Days like that symbolise working for *TMS* because it's just such great fun.

TOP LIST

Most defiant tail-ender

AGGERS Graham Onions. He saved two Tests in South Africa against all odds.

TUFFERS Easy. Danny 'The Duckman' Morrison. Along with Nathan Astle, he defied us for two-and-a-half hours and 133 balls during the 1997 1st Test in Auckland to ensure New Zealand got a draw. They had an unbeaten 106-run partnership, of which Danny scored 14.

ISA In the women's game, if you look at my numbers, you'd probably say me. Some of my innings were atrocious but they did at least last a long time.

EBONY Jimmy Anderson. Whenever he heads out to bat he knows he's going to be bowling soon. It would be easy to think: let's take a swipe and get on with it. But he loves hanging about. His record of 100 not-outs for England speaks for itself.

CARLOS Has to be Miguel Cummins coming in at No. 10 for Kent against Glamorgan in a 2021 County Championship match. Kent were 128 for 8 at the time but Miguel and Darren Stevens put together a 166-run partnership for the ninth wicket. Miguel's contribution to that was a single run. But, for sure, it was a run that mattered.

ALISON I've seen Nathan Lyon play many an annoying tail-end innings to get the Aussies out of a tricky spot. But for me it would be Jimmy Anderson. He's been playing for so long that he's got 100 Test not-outs to his name but the occasion which really stands out for tail-end resilience is his innings in the 1st Ashes Test of 2009 when he and Monty Panesar stuck it out in wonderful, agonising yet exhilarating style at Cardiff to secure England a draw and really irritate Ricky Ponting in the process. That draw was so important, it somehow felt like a win. England's Great Escape. I've also got to mention Jason Gillespie and the 200 he scored after going in as nightwatch for Australia against Bangladesh. If ever any Test batsman scores a maiden double century he still gets on Twitter straightaway to welcome them to the club!

AATIF Jack Leach. While the 2019 Headingley Ashes Test will always be known as Ben Stokes's finest hour – and rightly so – he couldn't have done it without Jack. He played a full part in one of English cricket's top five moments of all time.

INDEX

Agnew, Jonathan 12, 25, 49, 51, 85, 105,
    120, 154, 180, 209, 216, 238, 248, 252,
    264, 266, 290, 314–15, 316
JA's England debut, by PT 114
breaking news on *TMS* 271–4, 277–8
career change 125, 127, 130, 219, 305
England debut 110–13
incident with armed police 281
joining a club 35–7, 39–41, 42–3
on corruption in cricket 287
on his '70s & '80s 55–8, 62–6, 69–72,
    74–84
on his '90s comeback 101–4
on lockdown letter 262–3
on racism 41
on Allen Stanford 284
on *TMS* argument 222–3
on *TMS* spoofs & japes 295–313
on PT's England debut 119
on working at *TMS* 250–1
passion for cricket 3–5, 7–11
relationship with players 254–8
reporting on:
    Ashes *1990–1* 125–7, 130–1, 134–5, 140;
    1993 187; *2006–7* 149–50; *2005* 192–6,
    200–1; *2010–11* 152–3; *2015* 202–3;
    2019 2011–15
    New Zealand *1992* 142–3
    World Cup *2007* 149–50, 151; *2019*
    207–8
Akhtar, Shoaib 291
Akram, Wasim 25, 260, 265, 271, 290, 291
Al Hassan, Shakib 105
Alderman, Terry 126, 127
Ambrose, Curtly 164, 170, 172, 290,
    291, 306
Amir, Mohammad 288–9

Anderson, Jimmy 152, 196, 203, 205, 282,
    316, 317
Archer, Jofra 81, 207, 211, 212, 258
Arlott, John 3, 12, 229, 304
Asif, Mohammad 288–9
Astle, Nathan 144, 316
Atherton, Mike 115–16, 147, 160, 162, 164,
    169, 255, 256, 257, 271–3
Azam, Babar 121

Bagshaw, Baggy 35
Bailey, Trevor 255, 311
Bairstow, David 63
Bairstow, Jonny 212
Balderstone, Chris 56
Bannister, Jack 300
Baptiste, Eldine 111
Barmy Army 140, 173, 175
Baxter, Peter 127, 130, 221, 225, 228, 229,
    234, 273, 275, 295, 297, 299, 300, 309,
    310, 311
Bell, Ian 152
Benaud, Richie 15, 20, 59, 272
Benjamin, Kenny 164–5
Benjamin, Winston 102
Bennett, Don 89–91
Bird, Dickie 70–1
Birkenshaw, Jack 57, 101
Blakey, Richard 160–1, 162
Blofeld, Henry 205, 219, 227, 228–30, 241,
    281, 295, 296, 299
Bond, Jack 71
Boon, David 116–17, 118, 119
Border, Allan 34, 115
Botham, Ian 33–4, 62, 110, 111, 164, 312
    'Legover' 226, 306–7, 308–9
Boycott, Geoffrey 257, 295, 300–2, 304

Braithwaite, Carlos 22–3, 25, 48, 50, 51–2, 85, 105, 120, 154, 181, 238, 264–5, 291, 316
Brearley, Mike 33, 34, 58, 95–6
Bresnan, Tim 152
Briers, Nigel 101, 104
Bright, Ray 34, 72
Broad, Stuart 68, 78, 99, 202–3, 204, 205, 211, 212, 287
Butcher, Mark 170
Buttler, Jos 208, 212

Caddick, Andy 166, 254
Carrick, Phil 62
Carter, Jonathan 22
Chanderpaul, Shivnarine 181
Chappell, Trevor 34
Chauhan, Rajesh 311
Clarke, Giles 283
Clarke, Michael 152, 194
Clarke, Sylvester 65, 73
Cobb, Russell 67
Collingwood, Paul 196
Colvin, Holly 49
Compton, Dennis 12
Coney, Jeremy 209, 298
Connor, Clare 154
Constant, David 56, 111
Cook, Alastair 152, 202, 213, 248, 249, 250, 264, 282–3
Cozier, Tony 219
Crawley, Zak 258
Croft, Colin 56
Cronje, Hansie 173, 177–8, 256–7, 273
Crouch, Mike 125
Crowe, Martin 142–3, 144
Cullinan, Daryll 191
Cummins, Miguel 316
Cummins, Pat 211, 212–13

Daniel, Wayne 65–6, 67–8
DeFreitas, Phil 79–80, 81, 116, 146
Denly, Joe 212
Dexter, Ted 83
Dhoni, Mahendra Singh 120

Dilley, Graham 33, 34
Donald, Allan 173–4, 176, 177, 256, 273, 290
Doyle, Nancy 93–6
Dravid, Rahul 120, 180
Dudleston, Barry 71
Dyson, John 34

Edmonds, Phil 68, 89
Edrich, Bill 60
Edwards, Charlotte 49
Edwards, Fidel 291
Edwards, Kirk 154
Emburey, John 25, 89, 91, 92, 94, 97, 160, 162, 163
Estwick, Roddy 23, 25

Finn, Steve 205
Fitzpatrick, Cathryn 50, 290, 291
Fletcher, Duncan 129, 188, 195
Flintoff, Freddie 47, 149, 151, 194, 195, 200–1
Fowler, Graeme 78, 298
Fraser, Angus 68, 89, 98, 100, 116, 162, 166, 254, 255
Frindall, Bill 225–7, 295, 307

Garner, Joel 111
Gatting, Mike 67, 68, 74, 85, 89, 92, 93, 94, 97, 100, 120, 154, 185, 187
Giles, Ashley 188, 195, 196
Gillespie, Jason 85, 193, 194, 317
Gooch, Graham 49, 72, 77, 101, 102, 115–16, 118, 126, 127, 135, 136, 138, 142, 178, 243
Gough, Darren 25
Gover, Alf 36–9
Gower, David 25, 56, 62, 68, 69, 70, 73, 80, 83, 102, 110, 112, 115–16, 154, 159
  JA's dream captain 81–2
  handling pressure 75
  protecting tail-enders 73
  Tiger Moth prank 134–5, 136–7, 138–9
Greenidge, Gordon 111, 113
Greig, Ian 78

Grenfell, Joyce 4
Guha, Isa 17–18, 25, 47, 49, 51, 85, 105,
    120, 154, 180, 216, 238, 253, 264, 266,
    290, 316
Guha, Kaush 17
Guptill, Martin 207–8

Hadlee, Richard 77
Harmison, Steve 149, 192, 194, 254
Hartland, Blair 142
Hassett, Lindsay 266
Hazlewood, Josh 211, 212
Hayden, Matthew 181
Haynes, Desmond 89, 111
Hemmings, Eddie 132
Healy, Ian 185, 187
Hick, Graeme 97, 189
Higgs, Ken 62
Hoggard, Matthew 85, 195
Holding, Michael 64, 65, 111, 307
Hughes, Kim 34
Hughes, Merv 189, 191, 290
Hussain, Nasser 102, 121, 171, 176, 177, 178

Illingworth, Ray 4, 56, 57, 58, 62, 102

Jayasuriya, Sanath 162
Jenkins, Gordon 13, 31
Johnson, Martin 57, 103, 127
Johnston, Brian 10–11, 219–20, 221, 222,
    226, 228, 233, 236–7, 295, 296–8,
    299–300, 305, 306–10, 312
Jones, Geraint 195
Jones, Mel 46, 154
Jones, Simon 195, 196
Joseph, Alzarri 85
Joyce, Ed 277

Kambli, Vinod 181, 311
Kasprowicz, Michael 193, 194
Keating, Mr 24
Kelland, Peter 13
Kirsten, Gary 176
Kohli, Virat 120
Kumble, Anil 311

Lamb, Allan 68, 78, 110, 126, 136, 144
Langer, Justin 188
Lara, Brian 165–7, 168, 180, 181, 190, 254,
    255–6,
Larkins, Wayne 115–16
Lawson, Geoff 34
Laxman, V.V.S. 180
Leach, Jack 134, 212–14, 317
Lee, Brett 180, 181, 193–4, 196, 199, 291
Lenham, Les 31
Lester, Bob 17
Levy, Peter 8
Lewis, Chris 80, 166
Lillee, Dennis 34, 191
Lindwall, Ray 60
Lloyd, Clive 57, 111
Lloyd, David 'Bumble' 56–7, 102, 297
Luckhurst, Brian 74
Lush, Peter 126, 135, 136, 138
Lynch, Monte 79
Lyon, Nathan 134, 211, 212–14, 317

Mackenzie, Keith 299–300
Malcolm, Devon 116
Malinga, Lasith 291
Mann, Simon 281
Marks, Vic 83, 229, 255
Marsh, Geoff 115
Marsh, Rod 34, 116
Marshall, Malcolm 63–4, 65, 77, 111, 290
Martin-Jenkins, Christopher 134, 221, 228,
    229, 231–2, 242, 255
Massie, Bob 290
Maxwell, Jim 205
McConnell, Peter 116–17, 118, 119
McGrath, Glenn 192, 193, 194, 196, 198
McIntyre, Arthur 39
McMahon, John 37
McMillan, Brian 256
Millns, David 104
Mitchell, Alison 15–16, 52, 105, 181, 199,
    238, 245–7, 265, 275–6, 277–8, 279–80,
    291, 317
Moeran, Henry 235, 259, 302
Moores, Peter 284

Morgan, Beth 49
Morris, John 134–5, 136–7, 138–9
Morrison, Danny 142, 144, 316
Mosey, Don 221
Mountford, Adam 241, 242, 245, 250–1, 252, 259, 260, 267
Muralitharan, Muttiah 105, 106, 162–3
Murphy, Pat 222

Nawaz, Aatif 24, 25, 44–5, 52, 85, 106, 121, 155, 181, 238, 259–60, 265, 267, 291, 317
Neale, Phil 97
Newton, Laura 50
Norcross, Dan 155, 248, 264

Old, Chris 35
Oldroyd, Eleanor 311
Oliver, Neville 222
Onions, Graham 316
Ormond, Jimmy 188–9

Paine, Tim 212–13
Panesar, Monty 317
Parks, Bobby 63
Parsons, Gordon 69–71, 75
Patel, Dipak 97
Patel, Shilpa 234–5, 279, 299
Patterson, Patrick 290
Pietersen, Kevin 181, 192, 196, 199, 202, 314
Pigott, Tony 85, 100
Pollock, Shaun 256, 290
Ponting, Ricky 152, 193, 194–5, 197–8, 317
Pope, Ollie 258
Powell, Rovman 51
Pratt, Gary 195
Pringle, Derek 143
Prior, Matt 152
Proctor, Mike 302

Radford, Neil 99
Rainford-Brent, Ebony 19, 25, 46, 50, 51, 85, 105, 120, 154, 181, 238, 248, 250, 252, 264, 266, 291, 316
Raju, Venkatapathy 311
Ramprakash, Mark 89, 171–2, 188

Ranatunga, Arjuna 112
Rawling, Terry 35
Reid, Bruce 116
Reid, Winston 155
Richards, Barry 302
Richards, Viv 49, 70–1, 111, 114, 120, 180, 190
Roberts, Andy 62, 75–6, 80
Robertson, Jack 13, 29
Robinson, Ollie 112
Rogers, Chris 204
Rogers, Kelly 17
Roland-Jones, Toby 243
Root, Joe 180, 212, 257
Roy, Jason 207, 209
Russell, Jack 117, 119, 159, 160, 170, 256
Ryder, Eileen 4–5, 6
Ryder, Rowland 4, 6

Salisbury, Ian 147, 160, 162
Samson, Andrew 227, 301
Samuels, Marlon 50
Scott, Chris 168
Selvey, Mike 95, 126, 231
Shaw, Nicky 49
Shrubsole, Anya 247, 265
Sidebottom, Arnie 63
Skinner, Lonsdale 40, 41
Smith, M.J.K 146
Smith, Robin 126, 134, 136, 144, 185, 191
Smith, Steve 211
Smith, William 'Razor' 38
Snow, John 298
Sobers, Gary 256
Stackpole, Keith 58
Stanford, Allen 282–3, 284, 285
Stewart, Alec 39, 116, 117, 160, 162, 164, 169, 170, 254
Stewart, Micky 83, 93, 126, 128, 135, 136, 138, 222
Steyn, Dale 290
Stokes, Ben 207, 208, 209, 212–14, 264, 317
Strauss, Andrew 120, 149, 193
Strudwick, Herbert 38
Swann, Graeme 105, 153, 202, 245

Taylor, Bob 34

Taylor, Clare 50

Taylor, Les 71–3

Taylor, Mark 115

Tendulkar, Sachin 159, 160–1, 162, 165, 180, 181, 279, 280

Thomson, Jeff 60, 251

Thorpe, Graham 171

Titmus, Fred 39–40, 41

Tolchard, Roger 57

Trescothick, Marcus 193

Trueman, 'Fiery' Fred 82, 222, 224, 297, 300, 310

Tudor, Alex 85, 129, 245

Tufnell, Phil 25, 49, 51, 55, 66, 84, 85, 105, 120, 154, 180, 216, 238, 254, 259, 261, 264, 266, 290, 291, 312–13, 316

  JA on PT's England debut 119

  career change 241

  gets feisty/tantrums 117, 119, 127, 128–9, 161, 171–2

  joining a club 29–32

  mental health issues 145–8

  nightmare 'run out' 132, 134

  on JA's England debut 114

  on annoying Wayne Daniel 67–8

  on betting scam 285–6

  on his '90s 89–94, 97–100

  on racism 39–40

  on Allen Stanford 285

  on *TMS*, behind the scenes 243–4, 314–15

  on working at *TMS* 241–3

  passion for cricket 12–14

  reporting on:

    Ashes, *2005* 197–8; *2015* 204;

    World Cup, *2019* 209–10

  Test matches:

    Ashes *1990–1* 115–17, 118, 119, 125, 127, 128–9, 132–3, 134, 136–7, 141;

    1993 185–6; *1994–5* 145–8; *2001* 188–90;

    India *1993* 159–67

    New Zealand *1992* 142–3, 144

    South Africa *1999* 173–4, 176–9

    West Indies *1998* 169–72

Turner, Mike 43, 69, 75, 80

Tyson, Frank 'Typhoon' 58, 59–61

ul-Haq, Misbah 121

Underwood, Derek 105

Vaughan, Michael 92, 121, 149, 192, 195, 197, 202, 209, 249, 281, 282

Walsh, Courtney 164, 170, 172, 290, 291

Warne, Shane 105, 120, 180, 185–6, 187, 188, 189, 191, 193, 194, 196, 260

Waugh, Mark 132, 185, 188, 189

Waugh, Steve 51, 120, 132, 152, 188

Wells, Vince 104

Wettimuny, Sidath 112

Whitaker, James 67, 68

Willey, Peter 25, 62–6, 68, 75, 80, 104

Williamson, Kane 210

Willis, Bob 31, 32, 33–4

Wilson, Don 89–91, 98

Woakes, Chris 212, 262–3

Wodehouse, P.G. 6

Wood, Mark 82–3, 205

Woolmer, Bob 275, 277

Worrell, Frank 19, 20–1, 25

Wostrack, Jenny 19, 25

Yallop, Graham 34

Younis, Waqar 25, 271, 290, 291

Zaltzman, Andy 227, 259

Zaman Fakhar 312

ENDS